ICT Matters 2

Liz Hankin • David Sutton • David Dunn

www.heinemann.co.uk

✓ Free online support
✓ Useful weblinks
✓ 24 hour online ordering

01865 888058

Heinemann
Inspiring generations

Heinemann Educational Publishers
Halley Court, Jordan Hill, Oxford OX2 8EJ
Part of Harcourt Education

Heinemann is the registered trademark of Harcourt Education Limited

© Liz Hankin, David Sutton, David Dunn, 2004

First published 2004

09 08 07 06 05 04
10 9 8 7 6 5 4 3 2 1

British Library Cataloguing in Publication Data is available from the British Library on request.

ISBN 0 435 108344

Copyright notice

All rights reserved. No part of this publication may be reproduced in any form or by any means (including photocopying or storing it in any medium by electronic means and whether or not transiently or incidentally to some other use of this publication) without the written permission of the copyright owner, except in accordance with the provisions of the Copyright, Designs and Patents Act 1988 or under the terms of a licence issued by the Copyright Licensing Agency, 90 Tottenham Court Road, London W1T 4LP. Applications for the copyright owner's written permission should be addressed to the publisher.

Designed by Wooden Ark
Produced by Kamae Design, Oxford

Original illustrations © Harcourt Education Limited, 2004

Illustrated by Kamae Design, Phil Healey, Tim Kahane, Steve Lach and Melanie Sharp

Cover design by Hicksdesign

Printed in the UK by Scotprint

Cover photo: © Powerstock

Picture research by Debra Wetherley

Acknowledgements

Every effort has been made to contact copyright holders of material reproduced in this book. Any omissions will be rectified in subsequent printings if notice is given to the publishers.

Photos: ABPL/Karen Thomas page 95 bottom right; Alamy pages 131 left, 153 top, 156/Directphoto.org page 38 bottom right/Joe Sohm page 23/Photofusion/Alexis Maryon page 6 right; Art Directors/Trip/Helene Rogers page 5 bottom right; Corbis pages 6 left, 8 right, 42, 95 top left/Chuck Savage page 140 top/George Hall page 129/Jack Hollingsworth page 38 middle/Tom & Dee Ann McCarthy page 5 middle right; Cornish Picture Library page 116; Education Photos/John Walmsley pages 13, 140 bottom, 153 bottom; Getty Images page 5 middle left/Image Bank page 131 bottom right/Photodisc pages 4 left and middle, 8 left, 42, 74 left, 95 bottom left and top right, 143/Photographers Choice page 38 left; Harcourt Education pages 4 right, 42, 161/Gareth Boden page 170; Holt Studios page 5 bottom left; Rough Guides page 131 top; Sally and Richard Greenhill page 5 top; Steve Lovegrove page 38 top right; Trip/H Rogers page 8 middle/B Turner page 74 right.

Screenshots: Channel 4 website pages 43, 44 reproduced with the kind permission of Channel Four Television. FA website page 36 reproduced with the kind permission of the Football Association Limited. Flowol pages 140, 159, 160, 173, 174 reproduced with the kind permission of Rod Bowker, copyright holder of Flowol 2 by Keep I.T Easy (KITE). Flowol is distributed by Data Harvest. Google website pages 97, 98 reproduced with the kind permission of Google USA. HMV website and trade mark, page 36 are used by permission of HMV Group plc. HMV is a registered trade marks of HMV (IP) Limited (a wholly owned subsidiary of HMV Group plc) and is used under licence by Harcourt Education. Kingswood Educational activity centre website page 25 reproduced with the kind permission of The Kingswood Group. Mykindaplace.com website page 165 reproduced with the kind permission of Mykindaplace.com. Pupiline.net website page 165 reproduced with the kind permission of Pupiline.net. Science Museum website page 36 reproduced with the kind permission of The Science Museum. Thetrainline.com website page 128 reproduced with the kind permission of Trainline Holdings Limited. Thinks.com website page 128 reproduced with the kind permission of Thinks.com Limited. Uktickets.co.uk website page 128 reproduced with the kind permission of West End Theatre Bookings Limited.

Introduction

Welcome to ICT Matters

This is the second of three books designed to help you develop all the ICT knowledge and skills you need during Key Stage 3. We hope that you will enjoy the books as well as learning a lot from them.

The following information will help you get the most out of this book, so it is worth spending a couple of minutes reading it.

This book has five modules, each made up of a number of units. Each unit contains information and tasks for you to do, either on your own, with a partner, or in a larger group.

Each module begins with your Learning targets, these show what you need to do to achieve different levels in a module. Your aim should be to achieve the highest level that you can in each module.

Some sections of text and parts of the module tasks have a pink background. This text is aimed at pupils working at Level 6 and the high end of Level 5.

Each unit ends with a Test centre containing questions that ask you to describe, or perhaps demonstrate, some of the new things that are introduced in the unit. You can test yourself on the unit and can always look back at the content if you get stuck.

For each module there is an Assignment, which covers the same ground as the work you have been doing in the module. You will be expected to work through this largely on your own.

There are three types of tasks:

> Red tasks will take you quite a long time to do and will need a lot of thought.

> Green tasks are easier and should take less time.

> Module tasks are like mini projects that you work on throughout a module, gradually adding bits each lesson.

Introduction

At the end of each module there is a Skills help section. You can easily find these sections because they are printed on grey paper, they contain step-by-step instructions on how to use the software needed to do the tasks.

There are three different symbols in this book:

This means that you need to look at a computer file or resource sheet in order to carry out a task.

▶ *Skills help*

This tells you where to look in the Skills help section for help with a particular ICT skill.

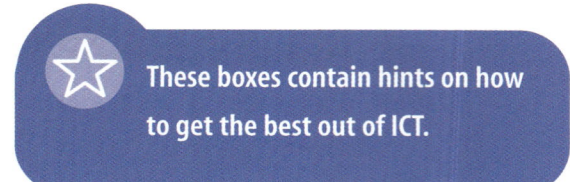

> ☆ These boxes contain hints on how to get the best out of ICT.

Hotlinks

Sometimes during a task you will need to look at a specific website. These are all listed on the Heinemann website and can be accessed by visiting *www.heinemann.co.uk/hotlinks*. When you get to that page, type in express code 8425P. You can then select the website you need.

Brief

A community website is going to be redesigned and you have been asked to help create a section of the website for young people, which can be accessed from the community website home page.

The committee working on the website wants the Young People's section to appeal to 11–16 year olds from different countries. They think it would be a good idea to have a web based game. The budget allocated for the development of the Young People's section of the website is £5250.

One idea is to base the web game around facts from the four countries that have links to the community:

- Australia
- Canada
- France
- Singapore

> **PLEASE HELP!**
>
> We need an interesting section on the community website that will make people of your age want to look at the website.
>
> We want a simple game that users could have fun with and that show links between our community and four other countries that we have links with:
>
> - Australia
> - Canada
> - France
> - Singapore

Developing towards the web game

In Modules 1–4 of this book you are going to carry out tasks to develop skills and gather facts, which will enable you to create a web game in Module 5.

Skills

The skills needed to create the web game will be built up during the tasks, particularly in Modules 2 and 5.

Introduction

Fact files

The facts you find will be stored as Fact files in spreadsheets, databases or web pages. The information in the fact files will be about:

- the types of music and bands that are popular in the countries
- likely names, height, eye and hair colour that people from the countries might have
- major cities in the countries
- details about schools in the countries
- distances that people have to travel to get from one country to another.

The game

The game introduces players to one or more Mystery Guests who come from the four countries in the game. Players are given clues about the Mystery Guest, which they must use to work out who they are. The clues will be based on the information in the Fact files that you create.

> Look at **Resource Specification**, this lists everything you need to consider when creating your web game. You will probably need to look back at this document throughout your work.

Contents

Module 1 Public information systems — 1
Learning targets — 1
1.1 Collecting and representing data — 5
1.2 Using and displaying live data — 9
1.3 Planning and creating a simple public information system — 13
1.4 Automating an information system — 16
1.5 Evaluating your simple public information system — 21
Module 1 Assignment — 23
Module 1 Skills help — 24

Module 2 Publishing on the web — 33
Learning targets — 33
2.1 The language of web pages — 36
2.2 Different ways of producing a web page — 40
2.3 Planning the structure of a website — 43
2.4 Planning the structure of a web page — 49
2.5 Designing a web page — 53
2.6 Evaluating a website — 57
Module 2 Assignment — 60
Module 2 Skills help — 61

Module 3 Information - reliability, validity and bias — 70
Learning targets — 70
3.1 Evaluating information — 74
3.2 Searching for information — 79
3.3 Structure of databases — 83
3.4 Searching for information using databases — 87
3.5 Data about people — 91
Module 3 Assignment — 95
Module 3 Skills help — 96

Contents

Module 4 Models and presenting numeric data — 108
Learning targets — 108
4.1 Using models to find solutions — 111
4.2 Developing a new model — 116
4.3 Using and extending the model — 121
4.4 Simulations and models — 127
Module 4 Assignment — 131
Module 4 Skills help — 132

Module 5 An ICT system — 137
Learning targets — 137
5.1 Planning a system — 141
5.2 Modelling a system — 145
5.3 Developing a system — 149
5.4 Using control systems to automate a process — 152
5.5 Creating an interactive control system — 156
5.6 Programming and testing the solution — 159
5.7 Marketing the product — 161
5.8 Developing and evaluating a marketing package — 165
5.9 Producing the project report — 169
Module 5 Skills help — 173

Glossary — 179
Index — 182

Module 1
Public information systems

Learning Targets

Input devices, such as sensors, collect information or data that can be used in systems.

In this module you will look at other ways that data can be collected and used. The module focuses upon collecting and using data that is constantly changing.

You will learn how to load data into a spreadsheet and how to choose the best way to present data. You will produce a public information system that will automatically collect data from the Internet and display it in a form suitable for your chosen audience.

In Module 1 you are going to learn:

About methods for collecting data including datalogging	See pages 5–6
How to transfer data between files in different formats	See page 7
How to create graphs in a spreadsheet	See page 7
How to copy data from the Internet	See page 10
How to use a web query	See page 10
About public display systems	See pages 12–13
How to use different methods for extracting data	See page 10
How to manipulate data displays for a specific reason	See page 11
How to create your own public display system	See pages 14–16
How to create a display to run automatically with suitable animations	See pages 17–19
How to evaluate and refine the display system	See page 21

What are your targets for this module?

To achieve a level 4 in this module you will need to   *level 4*
- Identify some systems used in everyday life which make use of sensors
- Discuss some systems that make use of datalogging
- Find some data on the Internet which is useful for your public information system. You will take data from several different websites
- Copy and paste the data from the Internet into a spreadsheet
- Choose the bits of the data which are relevant to your audience and bring them together on a separate worksheet using charts or graphs as appropriate
- Create a presentation which displays the spreadsheet charts in a way that is appropriate for the audience

Learning Targets 1

- Use some given criteria to evaluate your work and identify how you would make improvements

To achieve a level 5 in this module you will need to **level 5**
- Identify some systems used in everyday life and the types of sensors that are used in them
- Discuss the use of datalogging and the advantages/disadvantages in having automated datalogging systems
- Copy live data from a range of websites into a spreadsheet using a web query. Say why the data you have chosen is useful for your public information system
- Change your web query to make it respond to the input from a user of your system
- Select the parts of the data that are relevant to your audience and paste them into a separate worksheet in such a way that the source data and the display data are linked. Display the data using charts or graphs and explain what you have done
- Create a presentation that displays the spreadsheet and updates automatically when the data in the spreadsheet updates. Say why your presentation is suitable for the audience
- Set up the presentation to run automatically
- Develop your own criteria for evaluating your public information system. Make improvements to your system as a result of your evaluation

To achieve a level 6 in this module you will need to **level 6**
- Identify a range of different control systems used in everyday life and say how sensors are used in them
- Discuss the use of datalogging and the advantages in having automated datalogging systems in a range of different contexts
- Identify the data requirements for a public information system. Copy relevant live data from a range of websites into a spreadsheet, using a web query that responds to the input from a user of your system.
- Select the relevant parts of the data and paste them into a separate worksheet in such a way that the source data and the display data are linked. Display the data using appropriate charts or graphs and explain your choice of display
- Make your system more suitable for inexperienced operators by use of automated features, such as drop down menus.
- Create an appropriate presentation that displays the spreadsheet and updates automatically when the data in the spreadsheet updates
- Add animation and timing intervals to your presentation to make it run more efficiently. Set up the presentation to run automatically
- Develop your own criteria for evaluating your public information system, taking into account the needs of the end user. Make improvements to your system as a result of your evaluation

Learning Targets 1

What do you know already?

Presentation

A presentation uses text, colour and images to get a message across to an **audience** for a particular **purpose**.

Audience. The people who will look at or use something.

Purpose. The reason for making something appear as it does, or happen in a certain way.

Spreadsheet

A spreadsheet is a type of software that can carry out lots of calculations at the same time. It is a table made up of rows, columns and cells. Graphs and **charts** can be produced from the data in the spreadsheet.

Charts. These display data graphically so that it is easier to understand. There are different sorts of charts, such as line graphs and pie charts. Data are plotted on the **x and y axes**.

X and y axes. The x axis shows what you are measuring, the y axis shows your measurements.

Internet

The Internet is a massive network of computers connected together by the World Wide Web (www). The World Wide Web is made up of lots of **websites**. The Internet and individual websites can be **searched** for information.

Website. A website consists of a home page and a number of web pages that are about the same subject. Some websites sell things, others provide information, and some are just for fun.

Search. You can search the World Wide Web or a website for a particular piece of information by typing in a key word. The computer then finds all the appearances of this key word.

Sensors

Sensors are devices used to record physical changes and to send signals to a computer interface. Sensors include touch sensors, light sensors, heat sensors, sound sensors and humidity sensors.

Datalogging

Datalogging captures and measures data from a sensor. Datalogging software **automatically** measures data.

Automatic. Something that happens without the help of a human being.

Logging interval. The length of time between each measurement from a sensor.

Logging period. The total length of time during which measurements are made.

Logged data. Data that has been logged is presented in numeric form, it is usually imported into a spreadsheet for analysis, charting or graphing.

Learning Targets 1

Task

To make sure that you are ready to carry out the tasks in this module you need to know about copying information from the Internet and understand what is meant by extracting data.

1. Open a word processing program and set up a table like the one shown below to record four main celebrations that we have each year and the month in which they happen. One has been done for you.

2. Use clip art or search the Internet to find an image that is suitable for each celebration. Paste the images into the table.

Celebration	Month	Image
Halloween	October	

3. Select the table.
4. Go to **Edit** and click **Copy**.
5. Open a spreadsheet program and a new worksheet.
6. Click in the top left-hand cell.
7. Go to **Edit** and click **Paste**.
8. Save and close your work.

Unit 1.1
Collecting and representing data

In this unit you will look at some of the ways in which data can be collected. You will learn to transfer data between files in different formats, and use charts and graphs to help you interpret data.

Collecting data

Data can be collected in different forms.

- Manually using data collection forms.
- By searching data sources such as the Internet or CD-ROMs.
- Through the use of **datalogging** equipment, including **remote datalogging** and **remote sensors**.

Task 1

Open **Resource 1.1 Sensors**.

1. Think of five applications that could use sensors to collect **physical data** that can be processed later.
2. Which sensor would you use in each application?

Unit 1.1

Datalogging

Datalogging software automates the measurement of data. This has many benefits. Computers don't get tired, make mistakes, or get bored. Datalogging equipment can also operate in places where it is unsafe for humans to go. This uses remote datalogging systems and sensors.

So computer control systems are good at the boring, repetitive and dangerous tasks, and humans are much better at jobs that require imaginative thinking, creativity and artistic skills.

To ensure that you don't collect more data than you can manage it is important to identify the period of time you need to collect data for, and the interval between each reading.

Task 2

If you were automating a CCTV security system, what time gap would you set the camera to take pictures at?

Give reasons for your answer.

Case study

Here are two examples that you might not realise involve datalogging.

Example 1

Example 2

The company SSE provide sound systems to all the major music events, like the V Festival concerts and Top of the Pops. The law requires that SSE employ a person who continually **monitors** the sound levels to ensure that the audience is not put at risk. If you were to create an automated datalogging system what time interval would you set between each reading, and how long would you monitor the sound for?

Security companies often use CCTV cameras to monitor buildings. Taking pictures and storing the data requires large storage systems. So it is important to minimise the amount of data captured.

Storing data

Data is often stored in a CSV file type. CSV stands for **C**omma **S**eparated **V**alues. This means text and/or numbers are stored with a comma separating each item of data. It is a simple file structure that can be read by most spreadsheet and database applications, and is used when data needs to be transferred from one application to another. This file format is also known as a **length delimited file**.

For example, this is how part of a CSV data set about fish might look.

`goldfish,red,25,cod,black,100,guppy,multi,5,whale,black,10000`

Transferring data in this way is quick and reliable.

Presenting data

Data only becomes really useful when it is presented in ways that make it easy to understand. Graphs are one way of presenting complex data. Sets of data can be graphed in different ways, for example pie charts, bar charts and line graphs.

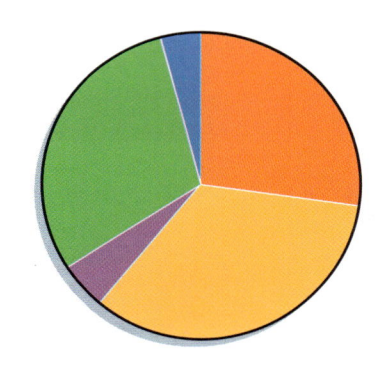

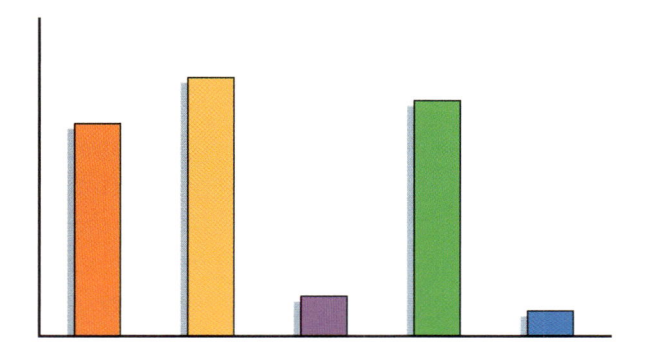

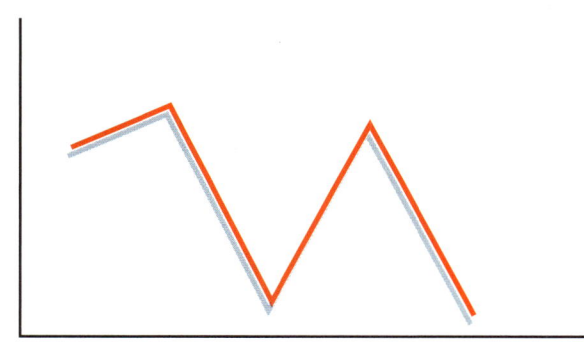

Line graphs should only be used if each point of the line has a value. Bar and pie charts are used where one data set does not necessarily have a relationship with another data set.

Unit 1.1

Module Task

A group of different sportsmen and women were asked to wear a heart beat monitor whilst playing their particular game or sport.

The data collected has been stored as three CSV files:

Filename	Total sampling time
Resource 1.1 Sport 1	4.5 minutes
Resource 1.1 Sport 2	50 seconds
Resource 1.1 Sport 3	60 seconds

1. Open a spreadsheet program such as MS Excel.
2. Open each CSV file and save it as an .xls file.
3. Decide which type of graph or chart should be used to display these data sets. Note your decision and give your reasons.
4. Create a graph or chart for each data set.

Task 3

Open the .xls files from the Module task.

Discuss with a partner the features of the graphs and the type of physical activity the sportsperson might have been doing. For example, is the person running steadily or sprinting? Are they at rest?

Test centre

1. What is a CSV file?
2. What is a data set?
3. a) When should a line graph be used?
   b) When should a bar or pie chart be used?

▶ Skills help

Importing CSV files into a spreadsheet, page 24.

Creating charts in a spreadsheet, pages 27–28.

Task 4

Open the two CSV files **Resource 1.1 Sport 4** and **Resource 1.1 Sport 5**. The total sampling times are given below.

Filename	Total sampling time
Resource 1.1 Sport 4	2 minutes
Resource 1.1 Sport 5	90 seconds

1. Save the two files as .xls files and create graphs or charts from the data as before.
2. Use text boxes and arrows to label the main features of the graphs to indicate what you think each sportsperson was doing at that stage in the data set.
3. State which of the sports listed below you think the person was involved in and justify your choice.
   - football or rugby
   - chess
   - archery
   - fly fishing
   - sprinting

Task 5

Explain why having data sets of heart rates from successful sportsmen made available to the public could help other people in their sport.

Unit 1.2
Using and displaying live data

In this unit you are going to learn how to access and use data collected directly from the Internet to make an information system.

Data from the Internet

The Internet is an important source of **live data** and information. It is very good for rapidly changing information like weather **forecasts**, stocks and shares, and the news.

However, caution is needed when using data from the Internet. Anyone can publish information on the Internet, so it is important you check that the data you use is reliable and accurate. You will look at validating data in Module 3.

The Internet contains an enormous amount of information that can easily be transferred to data handling software such as MS Excel or Access. Once the data has been moved into the data handling package, it can be edited and presented in graphic form.

'What's a URL'

'Unified resource locator'

'Wish I hadn't asked.'

▶ **Skills help**
Using favourites, page 27.

Task 1

1. Use search engines like www.google.co.uk *and* www.altavista.com *to find websites that show the music charts for the four countries in the web game:*
   - Canada
   - France
   - Australia
   - Singapore

2. *Copy and paste the URL of any useful site into a word document so it can be used later, or save it in your favourites. Find at least two websites for each country.*

3. *Check that the websites you have selected are reliable. You also need to check that they are stable, in other words are they likely to remain online for some time to come? It's a bit of a waste of time if you link up to them and they disappear! In general, the most reliable and stable sites are likely to be produced by:*
   - national broadcasting companies
   - national newspapers
   - government organisations
   - sites that carry government or trade association approval
   - companies that do not have commercial interests in the music industry.

9

Unit 1.2

Extracting the data

Information from tables on web pages can be copied and pasted into a spreadsheet. This is called extracting data. The data can then be edited or used to create graphs and charts. Sometimes more information than is needed may be copied. However the extra data can be deleted from the worksheet.

Module Task

In this task you will extract data from websites to create Top 10 Singles music charts for the four countries.

1. Create an empty spreadsheet file that has four worksheets, one for each web game country. Save the file with the file name **FourCountries-RawData.xls**.

2. Rename each worksheet with the country's name (France, Australia, Canada, Singapore). Save the file.

3. Go to a Singapore website you found in Task 1 or access one of the sites at: http://www.heinemann.co.uk /hotlinks. Find data that you could use to create a Top 10 Singles music chart for Singapore. Extract the data on to the Singapore worksheet. Either copy and paste the data or use a web query. Save the file. Repeat this for the other countries. Save the file.

4. Format and edit the Singapore spreadsheet so that the data is displayed as clearly as possible. Label it as 'Singapore Top 10 Singles'. Save the file as **FourCountries-Formatted.xls**. Repeat this for the other countries, formatting the data to match your Singapore data set. Save the file after you have done each country. Close the file.

5. Comment on how easy or difficult you found this was to do. If you were selecting a website to extract information from, what features would you look for?

▶ Skills help

Renaming worksheets in Excel, page 29.

▶ Skills help

Copying data tables from the Internet, page 26.

Deleting data from a spreadsheet, page 26.

Web queries

Data on the Internet is updated regularly. Keeping your system up to date using the copy and paste method would mean going back to the website every so often and copy and pasting the latest information to your system.

A **web query** creates a live, or **dynamic link** between the website and your system. By logging on to the Internet the latest information from the website is automatically copied into your system. A web query is a more efficient way of extracting data from the Internet because you only have to set it up once, after that it works automatically using **live data**. However, you should check from time to time to make sure that the **URL** is still correct and working properly.

If you edit a spreadsheet after running a web query, when you re-run the web query the data will overwrite the old data, so your edits will disappear.

▶ Skills help

Creating web queries, page 27.

Unit 1.2

Manipulating data

Data can be manipulated to support a particular point of view. For example, the starting point of the vertical (Y) axis can be adjusted to make the difference between individual items look much greater than is really the case.

Look at these two graphs that show which car most people would like to own.

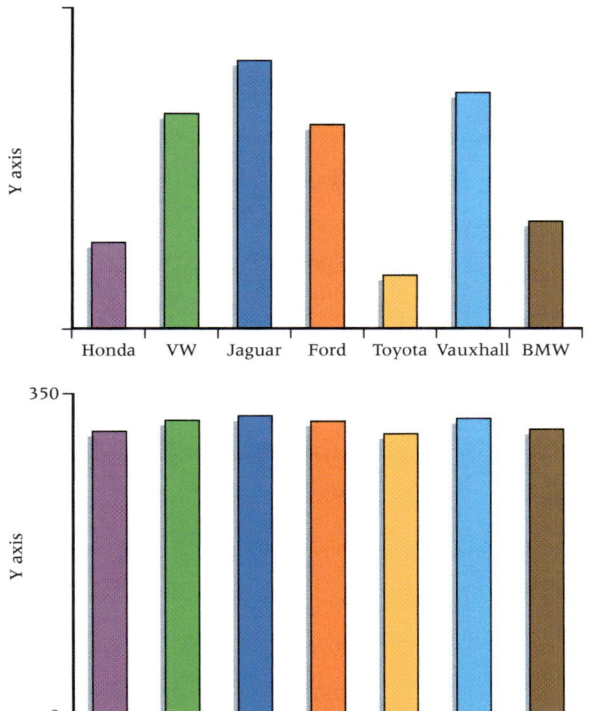

The first chart has the starting point of the Y axis shifted from 0 and deliberately shows no data values. The second chart shows the data in its true light. The same car is most popular in both charts, but it seems more popular in the first chart.

▶ **Skills help**

Editing charts, pages 28–29.

Task 2

Open **Resource 1.2 Canadian charts**.

This data has been extracted from a Canadian website which gives the album charts for several major Canadian cities as well as a national ranking.

1. Rename the file CanadianCharts.xls and save it.

2. Create a bar chart to show the national ranking of the top 10 albums against the Vancouver ranking, using the chart wizard default settings. Save the file.

3. Edit and format the bar chart that you have just created to make it more appealing and informative. Try:
   - changing the background colour
   - changing the font colour and style
   - adding a title
   - labelling the horizontal and vertical axes
   - editing the legend.

4. Save and close the file.

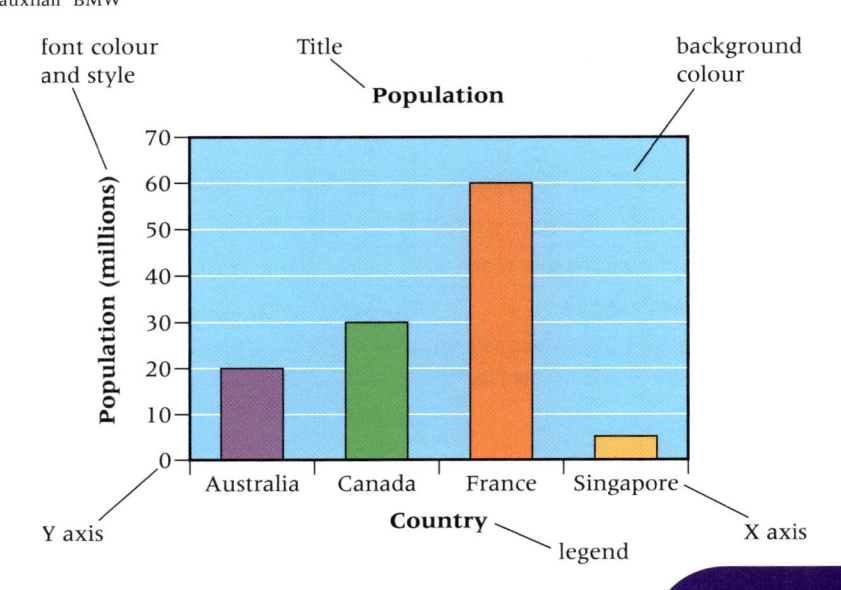

Unit 1.2

Using data in a public information system

Charts and graphs can be taken from a spreadsheet and placed into presentation software programs such as MS PowerPoint. The presentation can be used in a public information system. People sometimes manipulate the presentation of the data to get across a particular messsage, or one they think the audience might want to hear. This is sometimes calles spin doctoring.

Skills help

Adding captions and labels in PowerPoint, page 31.

Task 3

Open **Resource 1.2 Spin**.

1. Rename the file and save it as Spin.xls.

Imagine that you are a supporter of the music group Klimers. As the music chart shows, Klimers are in the lower half of this weeks music chart. You want to present the music chart information to show Klimers in the best light.

2. Which aspect of the information is most flattering to Klimers?
3. Create a chart from the data to promote Klimers' image, altering the position of the axes if it helps. Save the file.
4. Create a presentation for the local Klimers' fan club meeting. Create two slides. Copy and paste the Top 10 music chart on to one slide and your bar chart on to the other. Add captions to make as much as possible out of the data for Klimers.
5. Save and close the file.

Task 4

Open **Resource 1.2 Displaying information**.

1. Make a list of the ways that information, like music charts, can be displayed in different formats for different types of information systems, for example newspapers, TV, message boards. The formats could include:
   - graphs and charts
   - tables
   - text files
   - images.
2. State why you have chosen the format you have for your Top 10 singles music chart.

Test centre

1. What is a public information system?
2. What does extracting data mean?
3. What is a web query?
4. Which method of displaying data would you choose for information that changes frequently?

Unit 1.3
Planning and creating a simple public information system

In this unit you are going to plan and create a simple public information system for a school electronic display board, that can be regularly updated automatically.

Public information system

A **public information system** is a system used to display up to date information that people need or are interested in, for example screens used in a railway station, Teletext on the television or pages from a website. You will be creating your own public information system. The information system will be situated in the school entrance hall and will provide information for the pupils.

The information that is going to be displayed on your system is to be about the music charts from the four countries in your web game.

▶ **Skills help**

Renaming worksheets in Excel, page 29.

Task 1

In this task you will see if it is possible to create a combined singles music chart for the four countries.

1. Open your FourCountries-Formatted.xls file that you created in Unit 1.2.

2. On the Singapore worksheet add a 'Points' column at the end of the data set. Award points to each single - 10 points for number 1, down to 1 point for number 10. Save the file.

3. Repeat this for each of the other countries, saving the file after each country.

4. Insert a new worksheet after the existing ones and rename it 'Four Countries Singles'.

5. Copy and paste the data sets from each of the countries into this new worksheet, making sure each data set is labelled with its country. Save the file.

6. On the Four Countries Singles worksheet, create a combined music chart for all the singles that appear in the four music charts. Create a combined music chart of all the singles, listing the single and the points scored. Some singles will appear in more than one chart, if they do add up their total points. Sort the data by 'Points' to create the music chart. Delete all singles that do not appear in the top ten. You now have a combined Top 10 music chart for the four countries.

7. Save and close the file.

Unit 1.3

The Inputs

In Unit 1.2 you identified some websites containing data about various countries. This data will form the **input** to your public information system.

Processing the information

Once the data from the websites has been input into your system, something needs to happen to it before the public can see it. This is called **Processing**.

For example, you may want to:
- select only the most interesting parts of the data to show
- sort or rank the data to show who the best groups or teams are
- show data from different countries together for comparison.

Displaying data

Not all of the information in the country tables is needed for the public display.

An additional worksheet can be added to the spreadsheet to display just the bits of information required. This worksheet is linked to the other four pages and automatically updates when data changes. This is done by using **Paste Special** … **Paste Link**.

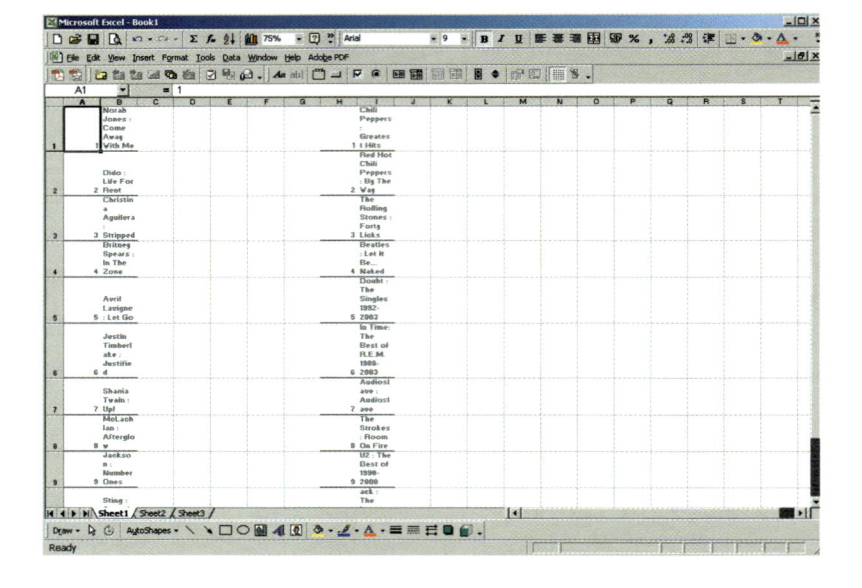

Outputs

The final **output** from your system is the information that the end user will actually see. It needs to be clear and easy to understand. For example, to make the information on the display page easier to understand you could create graphs or charts from the data.

Task 2

1. Open the music chart raw data file (*FourCountries-RawData.xls*) you created in Unit 1.2.

2. Edit and format each data set to create Top 10 Singles music charts for each country, which show the chart positions for last week as well as this week. Label each data set. Save the file as *FourCountries-Chart.xls*.

3. Close the file.

▶ Skills help

Copying data between worksheets, pages 29–30.
Using the **Paste Special** … **Paste Link** feature to link data between worksheets, page 30.

Unit 1.3

To make sure the charts offer a valid comparison between the sets of data:
- the axes need to be set up to have the same values
- the type of chart and layout must be the same.

Module Task

You are going to chart some of the data from the music charts you created in Task 2 and group them together.

1. On each country's worksheet, create a bar chart for the top **five** singles, showing their positions this week and last week. For fair comparison between the charts use the same set up for every chart. Give the charts meaningful titles. Save the file.
2. Insert a new worksheet after the existing ones and rename it 'Four Countries Charts'.
3. Copy and paste the bar charts you have just created into the Four Countries Charts worksheet.
4. Save and close the file.

Collecting data together like this is useful when it comes to finding data to put on to the display system.

Test centre

1. What are the input, process and output sections of a public information system?
2. How do you add worksheets to a spreadsheet?
3. How can you make sure that data in different tables or charts can be compared?

Task 3

If a public information system is to be used with a specific audience, the layout and style should be designed to suit the audience.

1. You have probably used a layout and a style for your bar charts that appeals to yourself and others of your own age. Experiment with your 'Top 5' charts from the Module task to produce two designs:
   - one to be used at a Star Trek convention
   - one to be used at a parents evening.
2. Insert a copy of the Four Countries Charts worksheet at the end of the workbook and rename it 'Style experiments'. Save the file.
3. Experiment with different layouts and styles.
4. Save and close the file.

Task 4

1. How would you choose to develop this public information system? Remember, it is for the benefit of the pupils and is to be situated in the school entrance hall. Write down your ideas and say why you have suggested them.
2. What software would you need to use?

Unit 1.4
Automating an information system

In this unit you are going to improve your public display system to meet the needs of the end user using presentation software. You will make a display that gives more information, which runs automatically and can be easily updated everyday.

Planning display screens

As well as displaying the music charts from the four countries, the system could display information about the artists in the charts. All of the information in the system will come from the spreadsheet file you have created and formatted.

To plan the information system, you need to work out:

a What data will be displayed?
b What will go on each slide?
c You will also need to consider:
- the background colour
- the font colour and size
- which toolbars to turn off.

Adding information

Using presentation software such as MS PowerPoint allows you to add additional information to a chart, for example captions. The captions could provide the following sort of information about the artisits and groups in the charts.

- Name
- Type of music
- Best records
- Age
- Birthplace
- Number of number 1 hits
- Number of music chart hits
- Publicity photographs

> The icons that appear along the top of any windows application are part of a toolbar. Most programs have several toolbars. The user can decide whether to display them or not.

▶ *Skills help*
Turning toolbars on and off, page 24.

16

Task 1

Open **Resource 1.4 Slide show**.

1 Plan your improved public information system for displaying as slides in a presentation program such as PowerPoint.

2 For each slide write down:
- a heading
- what information will appear on it
- from where in your spreadsheet the information will come

3 Open your presentation software and set up the right number of slides, with the headings you have decided on put into place.

4 Decide on a background colour, fonts and style, etc.

5 Save and close your file.

Automating the information system

Items of information about a chart can be displayed with a time delay between each one. This is important in an **automated** system – you will not be there to click the mouse every time to change the screen.

There are two ways of automating the information. You can either:

- select **Slide Show** on the top menu bar and click on **Custom Animation**

or

- by clicking on the icon shown or by selecting **Custom Animation** from the **Animation toolbar** (if you have it showing).

Unit 1.4

17

Unit 1.4

You can then set the time delay between each item being displayed. To help you get the timings right, so that people have enough time to read the information, you can record the time it takes a user to look at each page.

Once these timings have been recorded and saved they are used when running the slide show automatically.

Task 2

1 Use the Internet to find pictures and background information for the artists or groups in the music charts. Remember to record the sources from which the information comes.

   NB Check that the information is not protected by copyright before you use it.

   There are a couple of websites that might help you. You can find these by going to:

   http://www.heinemann.co.uk/hotlinks

2 Add each item of information or image to your presentation slides and then decide how each will appear. For example they could fly from the left or dissolve.

3 Set the slide show up using the **Custom Animation** tool.

4 Save and close your work.

'I think I might have overdone it, the words come in from the left, swivel, zoom out, blink and then go red.....unfortunately you can't read it either'

▶ Skills help

Automating your presentation, page 32.

★ Before you begin make sure you were looking at the display worksheet when you saved and closed the spreadsheet file. If you were not, the wrong page will be displayed in PowerPoint. The Excel file must also be closed before you start.

★ Don't use every animation feature possible, as it can put the user off. Decide on a style and use it on each slide.

▶ Skills help

Inserting a spreadsheet into PowerPoint, pages 30–31.

Setting up the slide show to be viewed in different ways

When a presentation is complete it can be set up to be viewed in different ways.

Will it be seen without a presenter? Will it need to keep on running in a loop, going back to the beginning each time? You can set the slide show to continuously loop in the **Slide Show** menu.

Module Task

1. Open your presentation from Task 2.
2. Record the timings needed for a smooth transition between the items on the slides.
3. Set up a slide show and check that it works as you intended.
4. Add a title page with any credits for where you found the information and details about the creator – that's you!

Something to think about…

What images do you see when the football results are shown on television? Are they the same each week? Do you often see the same picture of the Prime Minister or the Queen on the news?

▶ Skills help

Setting up how the slide show will be viewed, pages 31–32.

▶ Skills help

Recording the time each item and screen should be displayed for, page 32.

Task 3

Write down a list of five questions that you could ask a user of your system, to help you identify which other areas of interest could be included in your information system.

Unit 1.4

Broadcasters and newspapers keep a bank of resources to help them with the creation of news stories and newspaper articles. It allows them to respond quickly to breaking news stories. These resources include pictures and basic information about famous people and places.

Volatile information

Volatile information is information that changes quite frequently. The date is volatile information; someone's age is volatile information. Being able to add up to date information adds real value to a presentation, but remember – somebody needs to keep it up to date.

Test centre

1 What will happen to data if the command **Link** is used?
2 Why would someone use the **Rehearse timings** command?
3 What setting is used to set up a show to run continuously?
4 What is meant by volatile information?

Unit 1.5
Evaluating your simple public information system

In this unit you are going to evaluate your information system using criteria which you will develop.

Evaluating your system

Nobody gets everything right first time. It is a good idea to review the work you have done so far. To do this you need to decide what criteria you are going to use to evaluate it. You should look at the spreadsheet tables and charts, and the presentation.

Task 1

Open **Resource 1.5 Evaluation criteria**.

1 List the items that could be evaluated in the:
- spreadsheet worksheets
- presentation.

2 What criteria will you use to evaluate them? Here are some ideas to get you started.
- Use of colour?
- Type of information?
- Quality of information?
- Size and style of font?
- Speed of the presentation?

Plaza Hotel Evaluation Form

Why did you choose the Plaza Hotel?
_____

How would you rate the helpfulness of staff?
Very good ○   good ○   average ○   poor ○   very poor ○

How would you rate the facilities of the hotel?
Very good ○   good ○   average ○   poor ○   very poor ○

How would you rate the standard of your room?
Very good ○   good ○   average ○   poor ○   very poor ○

Are there any additional amenities you would like to see added to the rooms?
_____

Would you stay at the Plaza Hotel again?
_____

Unit 1.5

Task 2

1. Design a simple evaluation sheet for a partner to fill in. Remember to work out how to get the right answers to your questions. Can your questions be answered by YES, NO, or MAYBE?
2. Use your partner's evaluation to identify areas you could change.
3. Write a short summary outlining your suggested improvements.

Do the slides move fast enough?	Yes ✓	No ☐
Do you have enough time to read the information before the slide changes?	Yes ✓	No ☐
Is the movement between the slides clear?	Yes ✓	No ☐
Would you like to see more information on the slides?	Yes ☐	No ✓
How would you rate the appearance of the slides?	Good ☐ Average ☐ Poor ☐	
In terms of animations are there	Too many ☐ About the right amount ☐ Too few ☐	

Test centre

1. Why is it important to evaluate your system?
2. Why is it a good idea to ask questions that can only be answered by YES, NO or MAYBE?

Module 1 — Assignment

Exchange rates

To complete Module 1 you are going to set up a spreadsheet that will store information about the exchange rates for the currency of the countries that have been used in this module.

Background
Members of a local youth group are going to visit each of these countries and would like an up to date way to find out how much local currency they would get for a fixed budget of £500.

Brief
Use a search engine to find a website that gives you information on exchange rates. Now either use a web query or copy and paste data from the website into a spreadsheet.

Produce a chart showing the best exchange rates. Be careful, some agencies offer a very good exchange rate but charge a high commission rate. So work out the total cost of any exchange.

Create a public information system, using a presentation program, which would allow members of the youth group to check the exchange rates every day to see how they change. Write some notes about how you will keep this information up to date.

'Why does anyone want to exchange currants anyway?'

> A web query needs to be set up to update automatically.
>
> You can delete unnecessary data from your file.
>
> You need to set up the charts in your spreadsheet file as well as in the presentation software.

Module 1

Skills help

Importing .csv files into a spreadsheet

This is a sample of what a .csv file looks like when it is created as a text file.

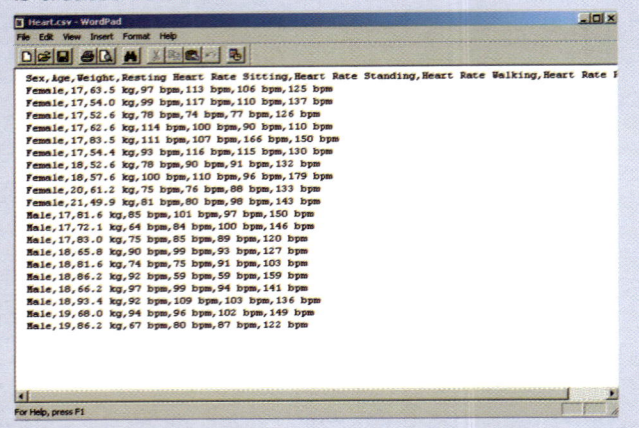

1. Open the spreadsheet software.
2. Select **Fil**e, and click **Open**.

3. Select **Text Files(*prn;*txt;*csv)** from the **Files of type** menu.
4. Click on the *.csv* file that you want to open.

The file will then open with each item of data in a separate row and column.

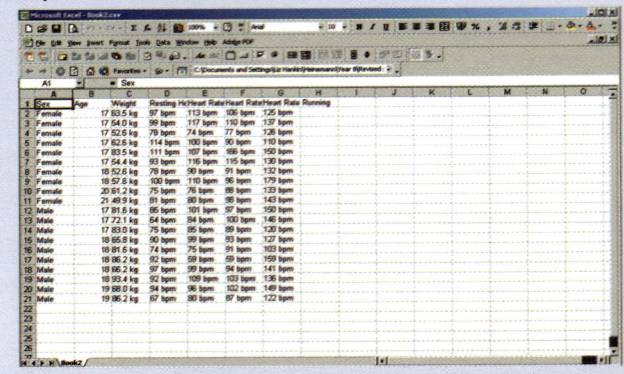

Turning toolbars on and off

The toolbars that are shown at the top of the screen can be turned on and off as needed. If too many toolbars are open at the same time, the screen can become very cluttered.

1. Position the pointer over the toolbars. Right mouse button click and the toolbars menu appears.

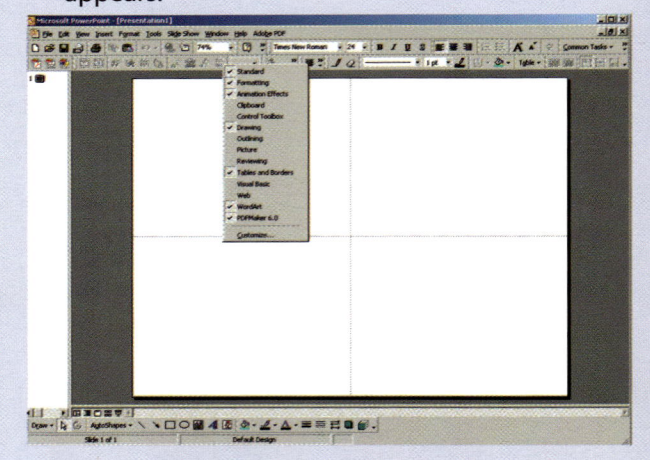

2. Select or deselect the different toolbars to display or hide them.

24

Skills 1

Using Favourites

Websites can be stored in a folder named Favourites. The website addresses stored in this folder can then be accessed by clicking on them, instead of having to type in the website address.

1 Open the website that you want to store as a Favourite.
2 Click on **Favourites**.

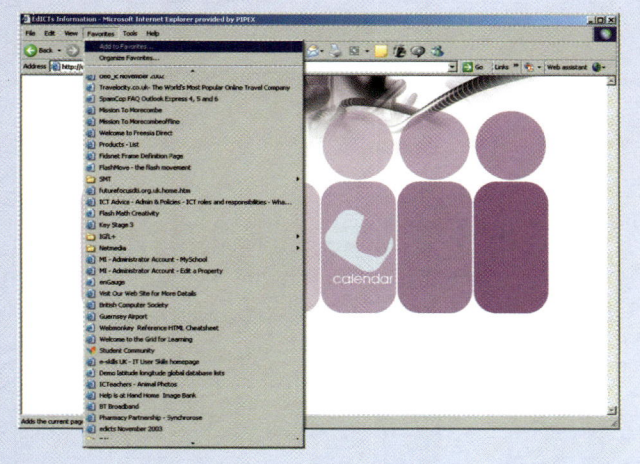

3 Select **Add to Favourites**.

4 Click **OK**.

The next time you need to look at the website you can select it from the list by going to the Favourites menu.

Saving web addresses in MS Word

The addresses of websites can also be saved in word processed documents. This will enable people who have a copy of the word processed document in electronic form to open the website directly from the Word document.

1 Open the website that is going to be added to a word document and highlight the website address.

2 **Copy** the address.
3 Open a word processing program and a new document.
4 Select **Edit** and click on **Paste**.
5 The website address appears in the document. Press **Return**.

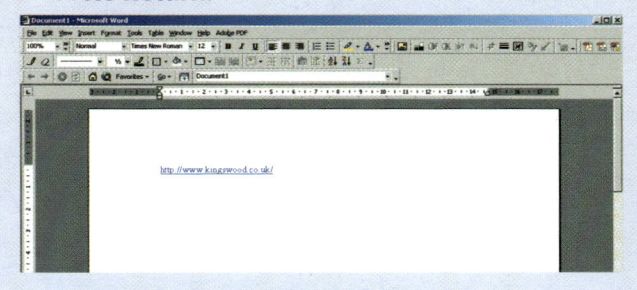

The website address will then be in the word document as a hyperlink to the real website. If it is not, then you need to make it into a hyperlink.

▶ *Skills help*

Creating Hyperlinks, pages 70–71 Module 2.

25

Skills 1

Extracting data from the Internet into a spreadsheet

Copying and pasting data tables

1. On the website, click inside the data table.
2. Go to **Edit** and choose **Select all**.

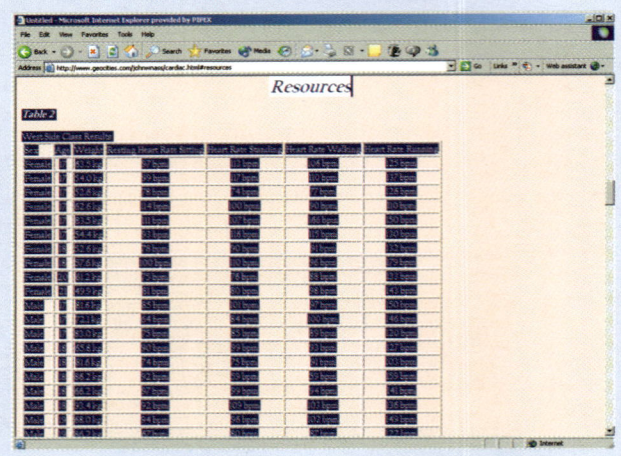

3. Select **Copy**.
4. Open spreadsheet software, such as MS Excel, and click in the top left hand cell.
5. Select **Paste** from the **Edit** menu.

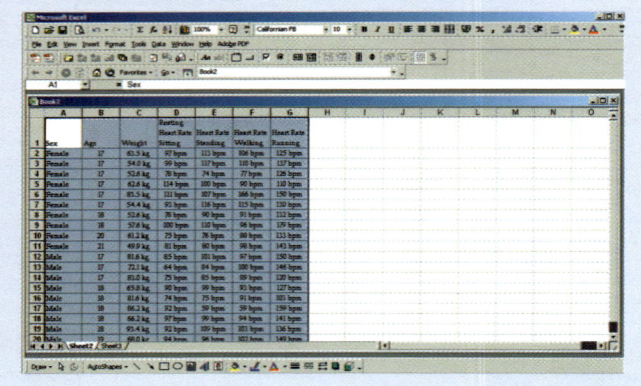

This may paste more information than is needed so delete the unnecessary information from the worksheet.

Deleting data from a spreadsheet

1. Click on the grey number or letter cell of the row or column you want to delete. The whole row or column should become highlighted.

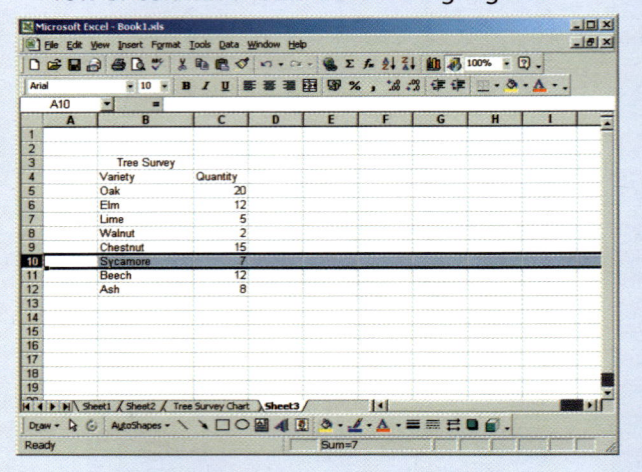

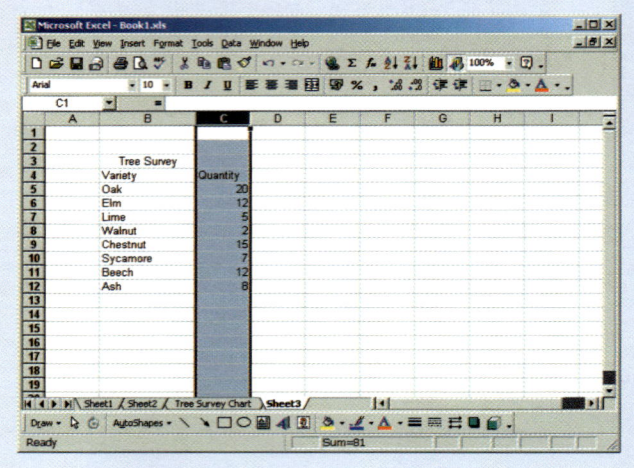

2. Click **Edit**, **Delete**.

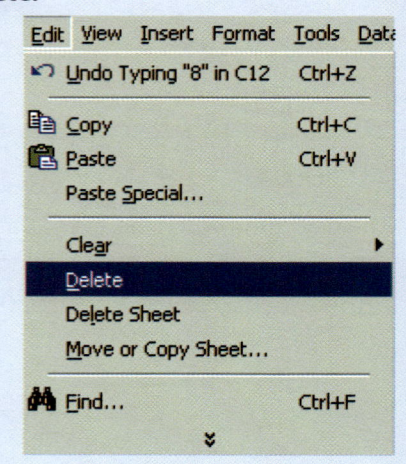

Creating web queries

1. Open the website where the source data is to be found and find the table that you want to link to.
2. **Copy** the website address from the address bar.
3. Open a new worksheet in a spreadsheet program.
4. Click on the cell where you want the data from the web query to start to appear.
5. Go to **Data** and select **Get external data**.
6. From the side menu select **New Web Query**.

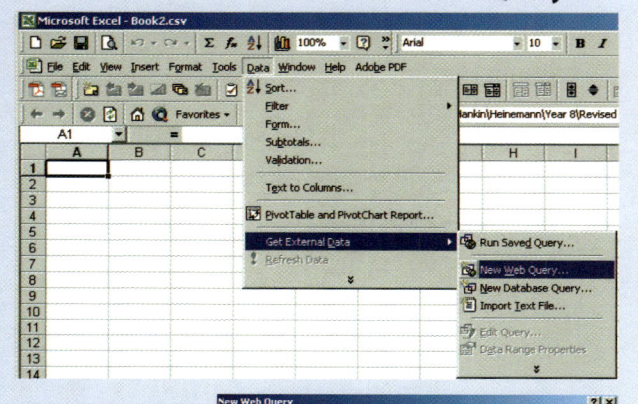

7. **Paste** the website address into the box and make sure you select **Only the tables**.
8. Click **OK**.
9. You will be asked if you want the data in the cell you have chosen. Click **OK**. 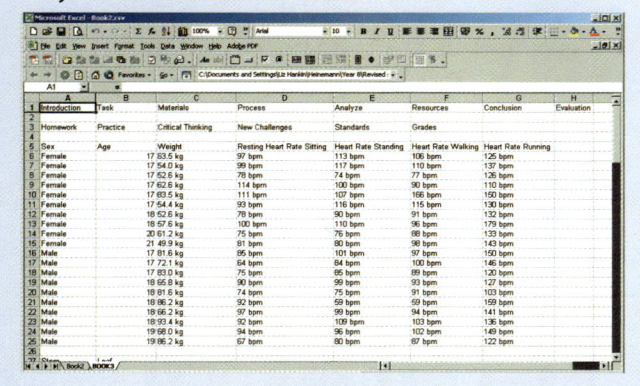
10. The data will then appear in the worksheet. You will have to edit the format of the worksheet to make it appear correctly.
11. The data can then be updated by using **Refresh Data** from the **Data** menu.

Charts

Creating charts in spreadsheets

1. Highlight the cells containing the data, including labels, which you want to appear in the chart.
2. Click on **Insert**, **Chart**. The Chart Wizard opens with the Step 1 dialogue box. 
3. Scroll down the **Chart Type** window and choose the type of chart or graph you want.

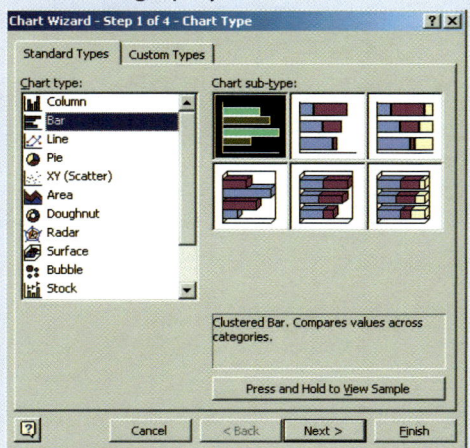

Skills 1

4 Click on the right hand side to select any **Chart sub-type** you want to choose.
5 Click **Next**. The Step 2 dialogue box appears.
6 Click **Next**. The Step 3 dialogue box appears.
7 Type a title for your chart in the **Chart Title** window.

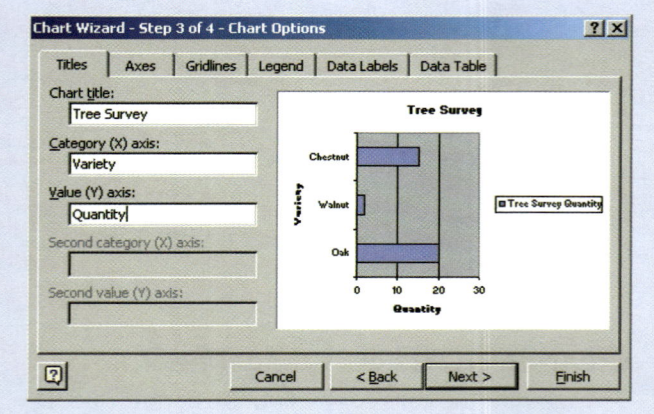

8 Type a label for the horizontal (X) axis in the **Category X axis** window.
9 Type a label for the vertical (Y) axis in the **Value Y axis** window.
10 Click on the **Legend** tab.

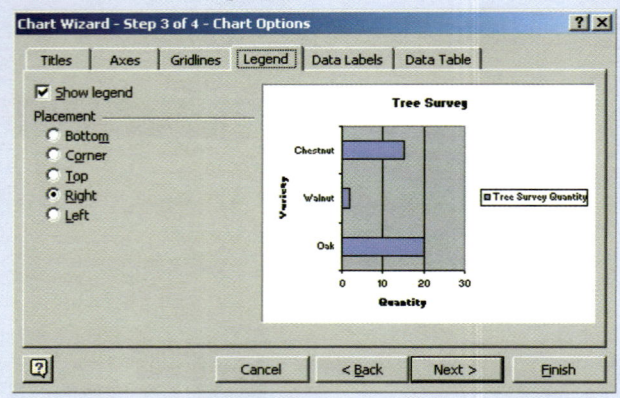

11 Click to select the legend and choose a **Placement** position or click again to remove the legend.

12 Click on the **Data Labels** tab.

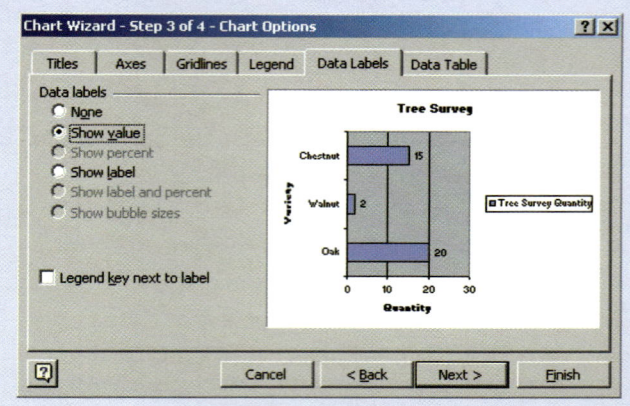

13 Click on buttons to choose whether to show value, percent, label, etc.
14 Click **Next**. The step 4 dialogue box appears.

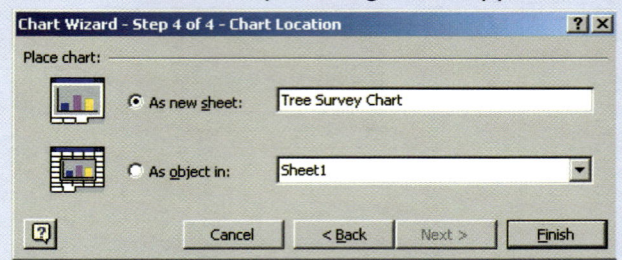

15 Click on buttons to choose where to place your chart:
   - To place it in a new worksheet, click on **As a new sheet** and type a name for the worksheet in the window.
   - To place it within an existing worksheet, click on **As object in**. Click the down arrow on the window to select which worksheet you want to place it in. You can click anywhere on the chart/graph and drag it to where you want it to appear.

16 Click on **Finish**.

NB: Depending on which type of graph or chart you choose, not all of these steps may be necessary. For example, pie charts do not require X and Y axis labels.

Editing charts

One dialogue box can be used for formatting charts in a number of ways.

1 Either right mouse click on the chart area, or double left mouse click on the part of the chart you want to format or change.

2. By double clicking on the chart title, you can give the title a border and a background colour. By clicking on the **Font** or **Alignment** tabs you can change the font and alignment of the title.

When the chart is being created, if the column heading is included, it is automatically inserted as the title.

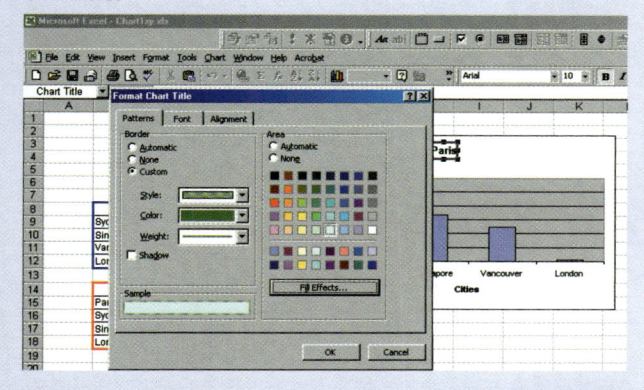

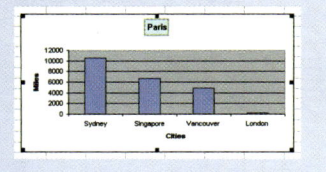

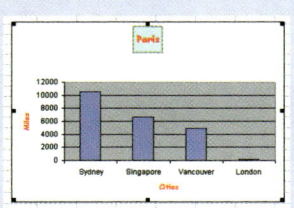

3. By clicking on the axes you can format these in a similar way to the title.
4. The chart can be resized using the resize handles to drag the chart to the size that is needed.
5. Double clicking on the plot area allows this to be formatted. In the same way the chart area can be formatted.

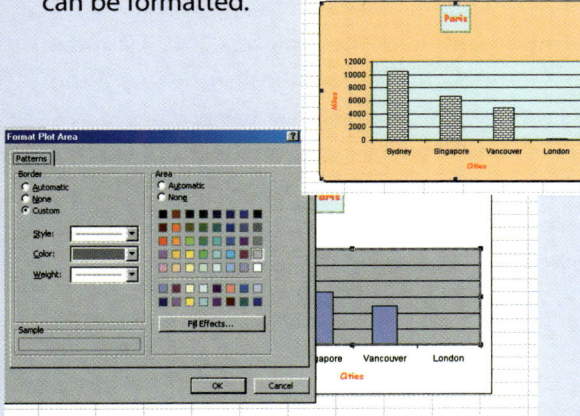

6. The X and Y axes can be added and formatted by clicking on the axes.

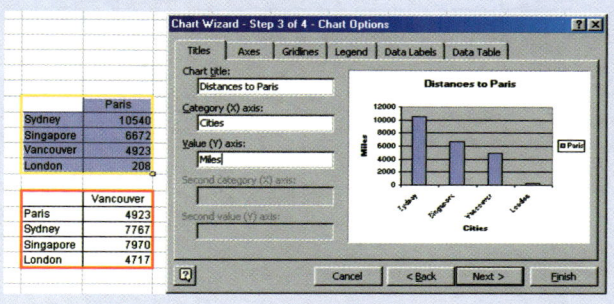

A legend is provided at the side of the chart.

Renaming worksheets

1. Go to the tabs at the bottom of the worksheet. 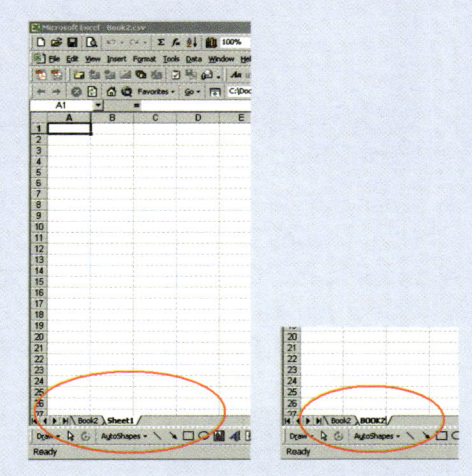
2. Double click on the tab of the worksheet that you want to rename.
3. Type in the new name.

Copying data between worksheets

1. Insert a new worksheet from the **Insert** menu or select one if there is a blank worksheet there already.

2. Move the new worksheet to the end of all of the other worksheets by clicking and dragging.

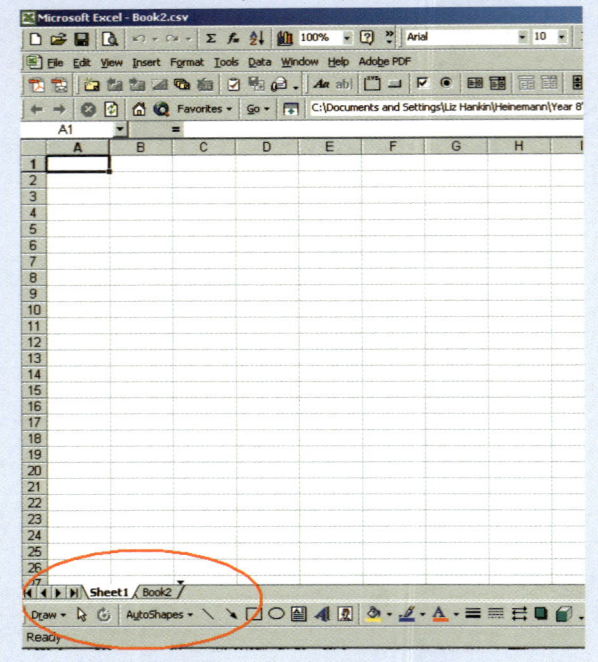

3. Open the worksheet that contains the data you want to copy. Highlight and **Copy** the data.
4. Move to the new blank worksheet and click where you want the data to go.
5. Click on **Edit**, **Paste Special** and select **Paste Link**.

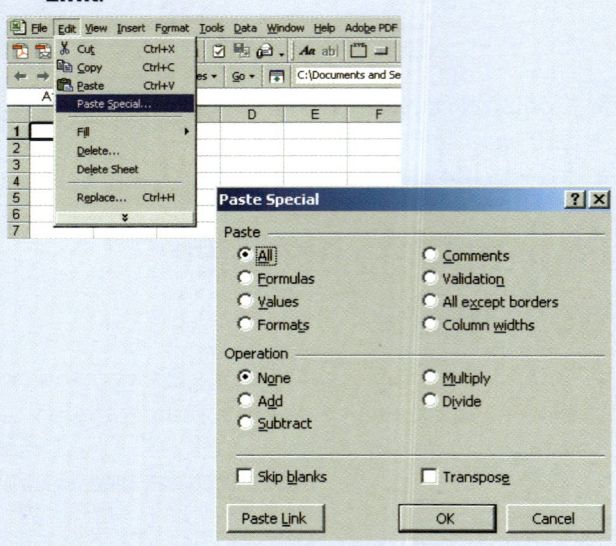

The data is now linked between these two worksheets so it will automatically update.

Inserting a spreadsheet into MS PowerPoint.

1. Open MS PowerPoint.
2. Select the **Insert** menu and click on **Object**.

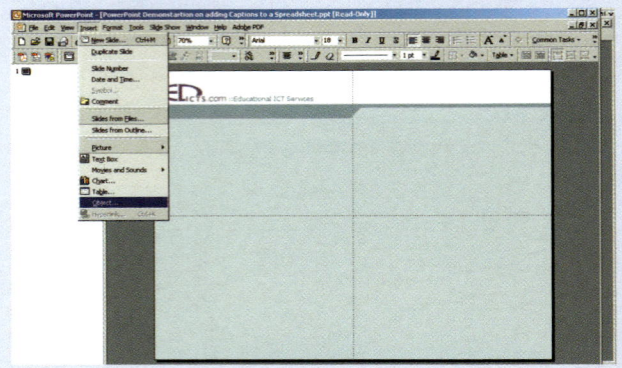

3. Check the selection box **Create from File**.

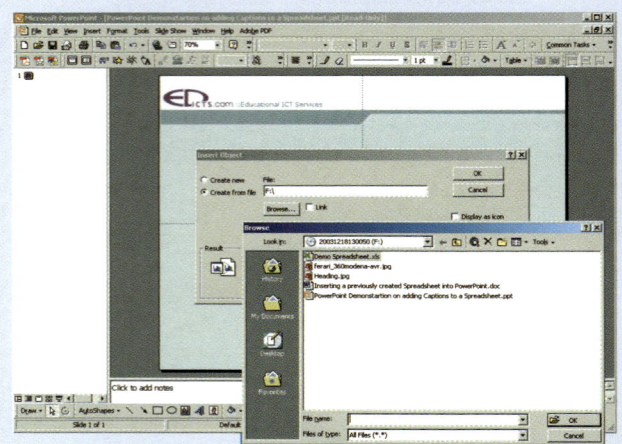

4. Use the **Browse** button to find the spreadsheet file you have created on the network.
5. **Important** – tick the **Link** box. This will mean that the page is automatically updated if the spreadsheet changes in any way.
6. Click on **OK** and the spreadsheet will be inserted into the current PowerPoint slide.
7. Reposition the worksheet, by clicking on the worksheet to select it.

Skills 1

8 Click and hold the mouse button down to move it around the page.

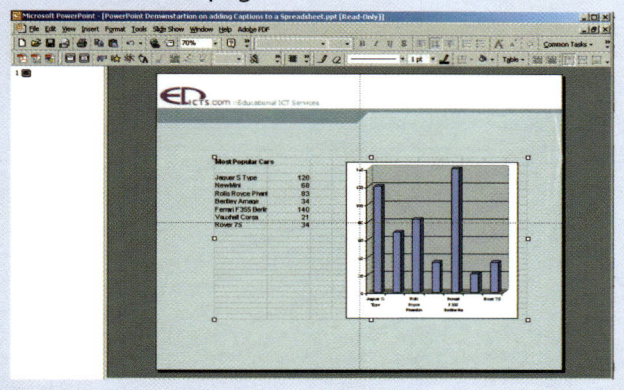

9 You can resize the worksheet by selecting the object and clicking on any corner handle.
10 To update the information on the PowerPoint slide, right click on the object and click on **Update Link**.

Adding captions in MS PowerPoint

1 Select **Textbox** from the **Insert** menu.

2 Click and drag out a box anywhere on the page.

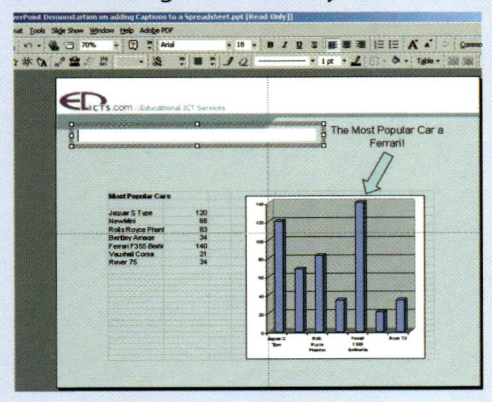

3 Click inside the text box and add your caption.
4 When you have finished click outside the box.
5 Move the text box to where you would like it to be displayed.
6 To add an arrow to highlight the key point select **Block Arrows** from **Autoshapes** on the **Drawing Toolbar**.

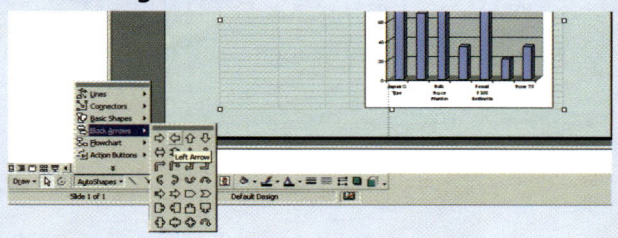

Setting up how a presentation will be viewed

1 Select the **Slide Show** menu and click on **Custom Animation**.

2 Highlight the object you want to appear first.

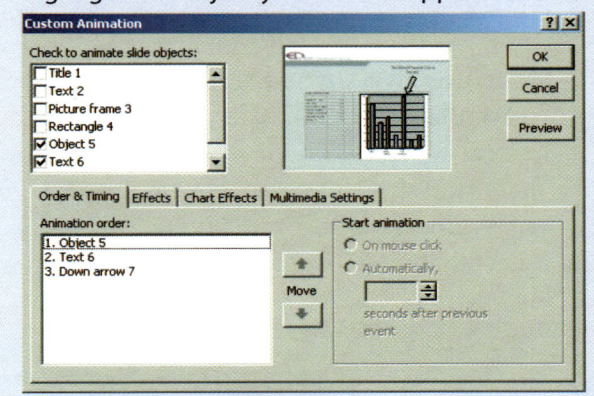

You can now decide the way in which the item will appear.

- The **Order & Timing** tab allows you to set the time interval between different objects appearing.
- The **Effects** tab allows you to decide how each object will appear on the slide.

31

Skills 1

3 Try out a few different options using the **Play** button at the bottom of the screen to evaluate the best option.
4 Highlight each item in turn and set the way you would like it to be displayed.

Automating a presentation

1 Select the **Slide Show** menu and click on **Set Up Show**.

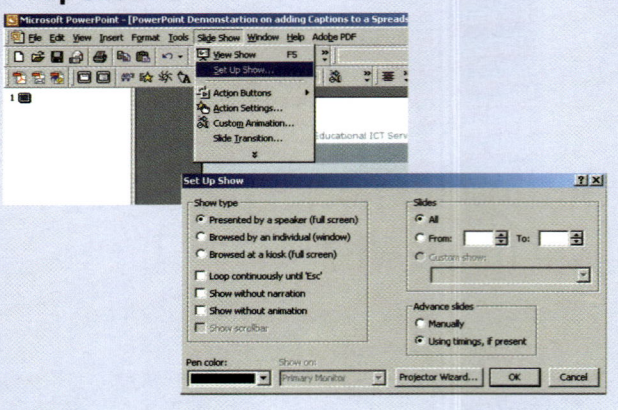

2 Select the settings that you need. To make it run continuously on its own, select **Browsed at a kiosk** and **Loop continuously**.
3 Click **OK**.

Recording the time each item and screen should be displayed for

1 Select **Animation Preview** from the **Slide Show** menu and check that each item in the slide show appears in the correct order.
2 Select **Rehearse Timings** from the **Slide Show** menu.

3 The slide show will automatically start and a timer window will appear.

4 Now use the mouse key or space bar to bring up each item. Make sure there is enough time to read each section before the next section is displayed.
5 When you have finished save the timings when you are asked to do so.

Module 2
Publishing on the web

Learning Targets

In this module you are going to design web pages for four characters that come from four different countries. You could use these characters in the website game you are going to create in Module 5.

The characters come from:
- Australia
- France
- Canada
- Singapore

In Module 2 you are going to learn:

About who owns websites	See page 36
How to use HTML to create web pages	See pages 37–38
About different types of Internet connection	See page 40
How to use different software programs to create web pages	See page 41
How to alter the appearance of websites, to make them easier to view or download	See page 43–44
How to plan the navigation of a website	See pages 45–46
How to create a hierarchical diagram	See page 47
How to use hyperlinks to link web pages together to form a website	See page 46
How to use tables to hold the content of web pages	See pages 49–51
How to use style sheets for designing web pages	See pages 51–54
How to create a site map	See page 55
How to evaluate and refine your website	See pages 57–59

Learning Targets 2

What are your targets for this module?

To achieve a level 4 in this module you will need to — level 4
- Evaluate a range of websites in terms of effectiveness using given criteria
- Plan and create web pages in HTML
- Add text and images to your web pages that are appropriate for the audience
- Discuss different types of Internet connections
- Understand that web page file sizes are different in different software programs
- Create a sensible way of navigating around your website using a home page and hyperlinks
- Plan and create the folders needed to store your different web pages and images with support
- Plan and create a hierarchical structure and site map for your website with support
- Use given criteria to evaluate your website, and suggest improvements to your web pages as a result of your evaluation

To achieve a level 5 in this module you will need to — level 5
- Evaluate a range of websites in terms of effectiveness using your own criteria
- Plan and create web pages in HTML, making use of different tags to change the layout and style of the pages to suit the purpose and audience
- Identify where different types of Internet connections would be used in different circumstances and why
- Explain why different file formats are used and select appropriate methods of creating web pages to manage the file size
- Create a home page and hyperlinks that provide an effective way for the end user to navigate around your website. Explain why you set it up the way you did
- Create and use style sheets, including tables, on your website, and say why the styles you have chosen are suitable for the purpose and audience
- Create a hierarchical diagram for the website and create the folders to store files and images in, and make use of a site map to locate files
- Develop your own criteria for evaluating your and other people's websites. Make improvements to your website as a result of others evaluation of it

To achieve a level 6 in this module you will need to — level 6
- Look at a range of different websites to see how they handle content and navigation. Use this information to help you plan and design your own website for the web game
- Plan your work on creating the web pages by breaking it down into a series of small tasks
- Create a series of linked web pages which include some automated features such as rollovers and navigational menus to make it easier for the user to find their way around
- Use ICT to improve the efficiency of your website for the end user, for example by converting and compressing files to make them quicker to download
- Test and refine your website using your own evaluation criteria. Create a response form on your site to collect feedback from users of your website

Learning Targets 2

What do you know already?

Websites

A website is made up of a series of web pages and a **home page** that are connected by **links or buttons**. The **owners** of the website created the site using **HTML** to display information for a particular **audience**. Websites can be viewed using a **browser**.

Home page. The first page of a website that leads to all the other pages.

Links or buttons. Used to move between web pages in a website, or to go to other websites.

Ownership. Checking who has ownership of a website gives you an idea about how reliable and relevant the contents of a site is. If the owners are an official source of information then the website should be reliable and valid.

HTML. **H**yper**t**ext **M**arkup **L**anguage. Programmers use HTML coding to develop web pages.

Audience. The audience is the people you expect to view and use the web pages.

Browser. Software used to look at websites on the Internet.

Task

1 Log on to the school network and go to the shared area. Find and open the file **Resource 2 Children's website**. Save a version of it to your part of the shared area. Give it a new file name.
2 Fill in the boxes around the picture of the web page with the correct words from the list underneath the web page.
3 Complete the sentences with your own ideas about the web page.

35

Unit 2.1
The language of web pages

In this unit you will learn about HTML and look at ways of evaluating the content of websites for an audience, purpose and ease of use.

So whose website is it?

In Year 7 you evaluated websites by using a series of questions like the ones below.

Audience or users	Has the website been designed for a particular audience? Is the content written so that the audience will understand and be able to use it?
Relevance	Does it give the information that the users want?
Accuracy	Is the information accurate? Is it **plausible** – does it seem sensible? Can you tell where it has come from, for example is it an official or unofficial website? Does it give information from different points of view or show a **bias**?
Quality of display	Have the web pages been created with text, colours and graphics that match the audience?
Validity	Does it seem true or **authentic**? Is there enough up to date information to make it worthwhile using?
Ease of use	Could a user find out how to use the website or is it confusing?

Task 1

Look at these three websites. You can find their addresses at:

http://www.heinemann.co.uk/hotlinks

Write down your views about each of the websites by using the questions from the table above to help you **appraise** them.

What is behind a web page?

Computer programs all use computer languages. Web page designers can use a language called **HTML** or **h**yper**t**ext **m**arkup **l**anguage. This is a code used to tell the computer where and how to display items on a web page. HTML code items are called **tags**.

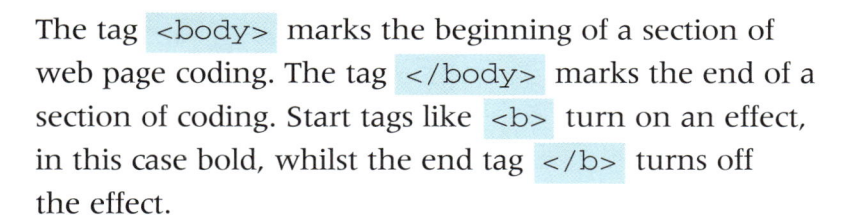

`<body>`

`</h1>`

The tag `<body>` marks the beginning of a section of web page coding. The tag `</body>` marks the end of a section of coding. Start tags like `<b>` turn on an effect, in this case bold, whilst the end tag `</b>` turns off the effect.

Below are just the start tags HTML would use to display the word HELLO as a heading on a web page.

Code	What follows is	Web page
`<html>`	A web page	
`<body>`	The coded contents of the page	HELLO
`<h1 align=center>`	A heading (type 1) placed in the centre	
`<HELLO>`	The contents for display	

The full HTML coding for the heading looks like this:

```
<html>
<body>
<h1 align=center>
HELLO
</h1>
</body>
</html>
```

Unit 2.1

You can see how the symbols are used to start and finish instructions. If you want to add more words underneath the heading you just write them in after `</h1>`. Since the computer knows 'HELLO' is a heading it will leave a space and put what you write on a new line.

If you want to start a new line at any time, you can tell the computer to go to another line by using the tag `<br>`.

▶ *Skills help*

Using HTML, page 61.

Resource 2.1 HTML glossary.

Task 2

1. Open the Notepad software.
2. Type in the HTML code needed to display the following information on a web page:
   - Your own first name as a heading, in bold, in the centre of the page.
   - Then underneath your name display three things about you, for example short, brown eyes, like watching football.
3. Save the file as description1.txt *in the shared area.*
4. To look at your file as a web page you have to save it as an .htm file. The .htm *is called a file extension.* Rename your file as description1.htm.
5. Open an Internet browser and then open the description1.htm file. Does it look like you expected it to?

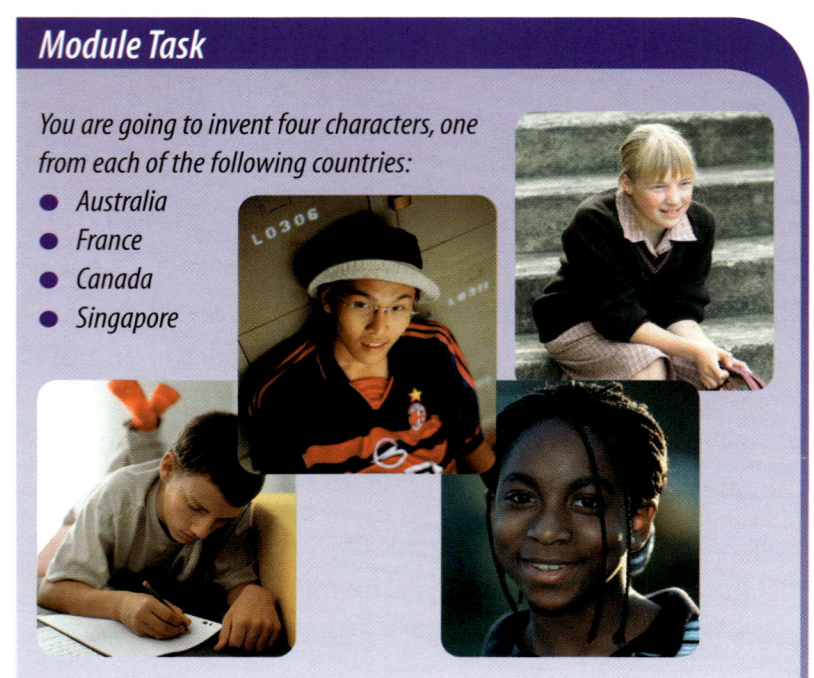

Module Task

You are going to invent four characters, one from each of the following countries:
- Australia
- France
- Canada
- Singapore

For each character you will create a web page.

1. Work with a partner to create the four web pages. Each page should have a description of the character giving the following information:
   - character's name
   - character's age
   - three pieces of information about the way they look – eye colour, hair colour, and height.

It might help if you create a **storyboard** *for the way the pages will appear.*

2. Create a folder called **character website** *in the shared area. Save the character pages to this folder using the following file names, make sure that you use* .htm *as the file extension.*

   Character1.htm   Character3.htm
   Character2.htm   Character4.htm

3. Use your web browser to look at the pages.

38

Task 3

1 Print out the four character web pages you have created.

2 Annotate the web pages to show how you would like to improve the way that the information is displayed, to make them more interesting to look at and use. For example you could make the character web pages more individual by making them match your ideas for the characters.

Task 4

1 To make the character web pages more individual and to make them match your ideas for the characters, find out how you can change fonts and colours using HTML.

Look at **Resource 2.1 HTML glossary** for help.

2 Change the fonts and colours of your web pages, saving them as **character1a.htm**, etc. so that you still have your original versions.

Test centre

1 What is HTML?
2 What is a web browser?
3 What does navigating a website mean?

Unit 2.2
Different ways of producing a web page

In this unit you are going to find out about two different ways of creating web pages and how they compare. You will also learn about the technical side of electronic communications.

Connections

When people talk about connecting to the Internet they say things like

- dial-up
- ISDN
- broadband
- modem speed

So what difference do these things make to how we use the Internet?

The way a computer is connected to the Internet affects the speed that websites appear and how quickly different pages in a website can be accessed. This might not seem very important if you have all day, but when you are trying to work with data that is constantly changing, such as financial data, time really does mean money.

The connection between a home computer and the Internet follows a standard pathway, although the type of connection might be different.

Task 1

*You are going to look at a website and find out about different aspects of connection, such as **bandwidth** and **transmission speed**. Access the website at:*

http://heinemann.co.uk/hotlinks

Make notes about the different types of connection, but don't copy it all down, make sure you understand what you are writing.

Open **Resource 2.2 Connections** and use your notes to complete the table.

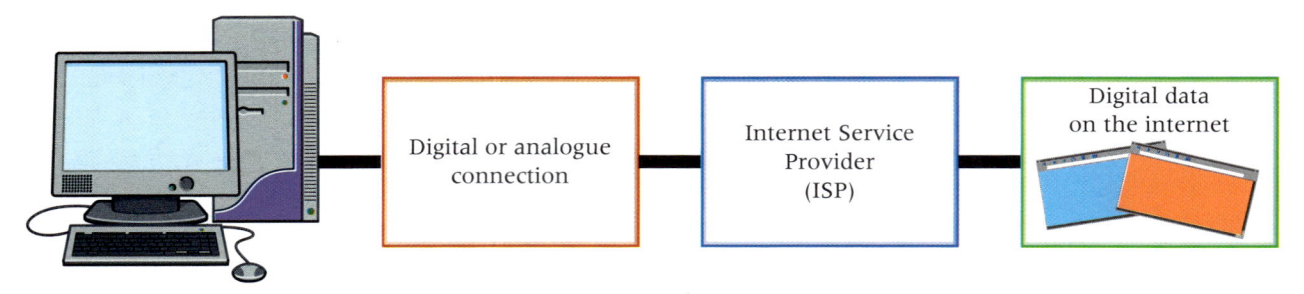

Home computer → Digital or analogue connection → Internet Service Provider (ISP) → Digital data on the internet

40

Two methods of developing web pages

To understand why using a computer language like HTML is important, you need to see the difference it can make in creating a web page.

Word processing programs, like MS Word, can be used to make simple web pages. The page is created like any other word processed document, but the file is saved in web page format (*.htm*).

One difference between web pages created using a word processing program and web pages created using HTML is that the **file sizes** of word processed pages are much larger.

What difference do you think this would make when a page is viewed online?

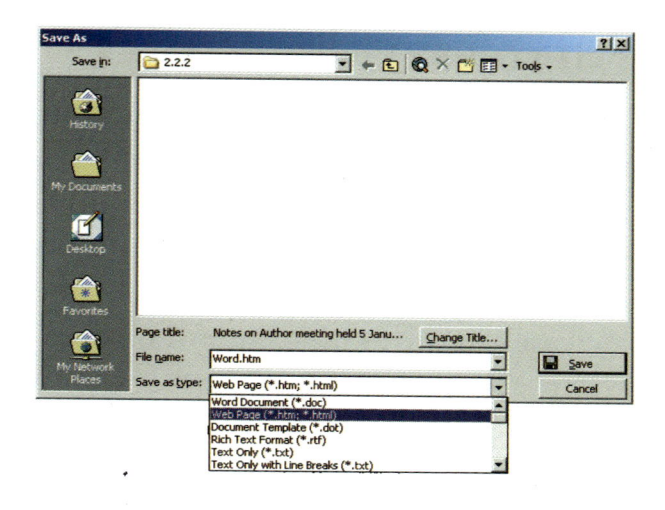

▶ Skills help

Selecting different formats of files when you save, page 62.

Finding out the size of files using file properties, pages 62–63.

Module Task

To see what happens to file sizes you are going to create the same web page in two different ways.

1. Open a word processing program such as MS Word.

2. Create a document by typing in the following information.

    - My name is David — Make this centered as a heading
    - I am shortish and have greeny-brown eyes — Make this a three line space / Make this the description
    - I like playing the guitar and piano — Make this a two line space

3. Now save this document, making sure that you select **Web Page** in the **Save as type** box so the file name is word.htm.

4. Open the Notepad software and type in the following HTML code, making sure that you get all of the symbols in the right place.
    ```
    <html>
    <body>
    <h1 align=center><b>My name is David</b></h1>
    <br><br><br> I am shortish with greeny-brown eyes<br><br> I like playing the guitar and the piano
    </body></html></a></p>
    ```

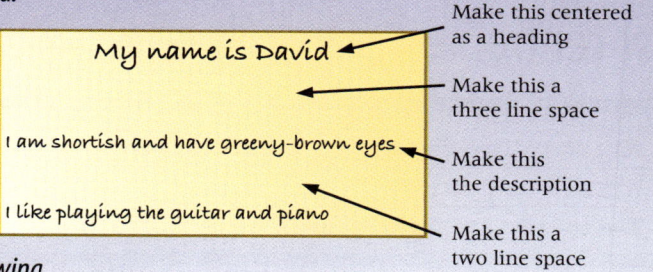

5. Save this file as Page 1, making sure that the file is called **Page 1.htm**.

6. Now compare the file sizes of these two files by looking at their properties.

7. What is the difference in file size?

8. What would this mean if you were accessing these web pages over a slow Internet connection?

Unit 2.2

Extra coding

Programmers using HTML coding will often add coding to the start of a web page, which is not needed to make it display properly. This extra code is designed to give the page the correct title and to make it easier for Internet search engines to find it. This coding can increase the size of files, but it is necessary to make the web pages more useful on the Internet.

You can look at the HTML code used by the programmer of a website by looking at the source code in a web browser.

Task 2

1. Open your **Word.htm** file in a web browser.
2. From the top menu bar in the browser click on **View** and then click on **Source**.
3. Find the section of the source code that is like the file you created in HTML.
4. Find out how much code can be deleted before it changes the way the page appears in the web browser.

NB Save edited versions with different file names to view them.

Task 3

1. Which method of creating web pages keeps file size small?
2. Which method is the easiest way for most people to create web pages?
3. Write a short report that tells someone who is new to web design the best methods for designing web pages for different reasons.

Test centre

1. What different types of connection to the Internet are there?
2. What is a file extension?
3. What file format is needed for web pages?

Unit 2.3
Planning the structure of a website

In this unit you are going to work out how users will access information about the characters from the web pages you have created. You will have to think about a home page and the information you need about your characters.

Website appearance

Websites are designed to be viewed with text and graphics visible. This can make them take a long time to appear. One way around this problem is to view websites without graphics, fancy fonts and animations.

Look at this screenshot of a well known website.

This is how it appears if you turn off the fonts and font style settings. The screen is clearer and it is easier to read.

▶ *Skills help*

Turning off fonts and font style settings, page 69.

43

Turning off the graphics allows web pages to load faster.

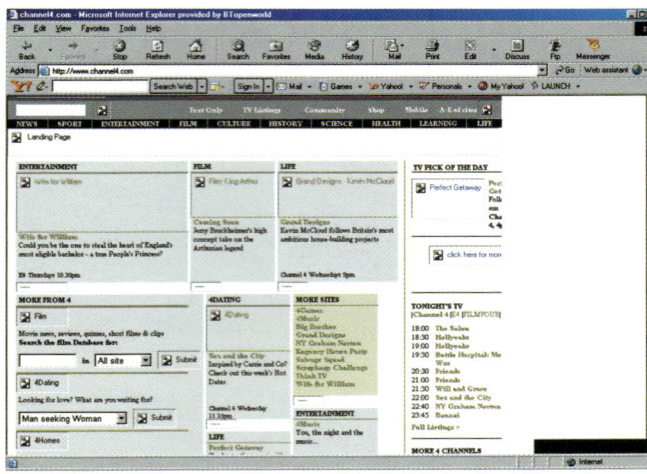

Some people who can't see very well need to see pages as text only. It is also easier for them to read if the text is displayed as light on a dark background.

▶ *Skills help*

Turning off graphics, page 69.

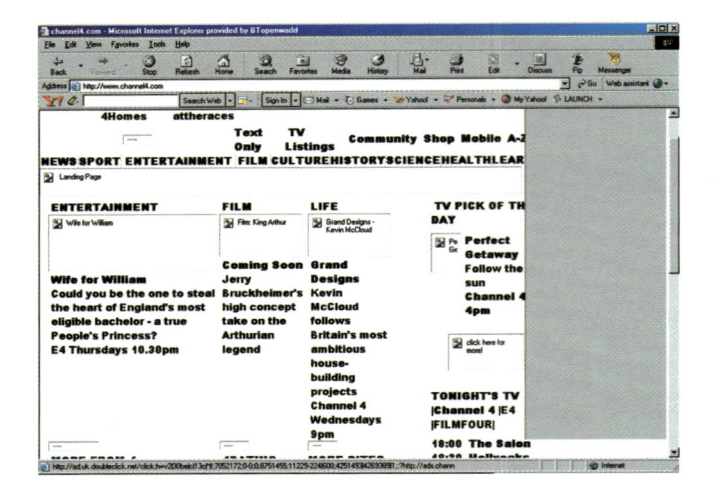

Building the information

When creating a website it is important to decide exactly what information will be needed on each web page.

You have already created web pages about the characters in your web game. These pages contain a small amount of information about each of them, but to make the pages more interesting you need to provide more information.

Unit 2.3

Task 1

You are going to create character Fact Files to use when creating your web pages. As well as the personal details you have already invented for the four characters, you need five further items of information.

Open **Resource 2.3 Sources of information.**

Create a table like the one below to list the facts about each character. You should already have details of the characters' names, age, height, eye colour and hair colour. If you wish, you can use the three further items of information shown in the table, but remember you still need to come up with two more items yourself.

Remember – you are inventing the characters not the facts. Make sure the information about each character hangs together. Their city **must really be in** the country they live in. The local band **must really come from** the country they live in.

Use the table to list where you will look for, or confirm, the facts you are going to use.

NB. The end column is for use in the Module task.

Items	Sources of information			
Name				
Age	not applicable			
Height				
Hair colour				
Eye colour				
City they live in				
Image of character				
Favourite local band				

Home pages

Good websites are easy to use, with information found where you would expect it to be.

The first page of a website is called the **home page**. The home page provides an introduction to the website, outlining what information can be found on the site. It is important that users can return to the home page from anywhere in the website. This can stop them feeling lost and wondering where to go. Moving between web pages and the home page is known as **navigating** the website.

You need to think about what information should appear on the home page of your website. Because you have four characters you will need to set up four areas on the home page, one for each character. You also need to plan the navigation to the different character's web pages.

Unit 2.3

Here are four possible layouts for a home page showing the different characters. People can find out more information about the characters by clicking on one of the links.

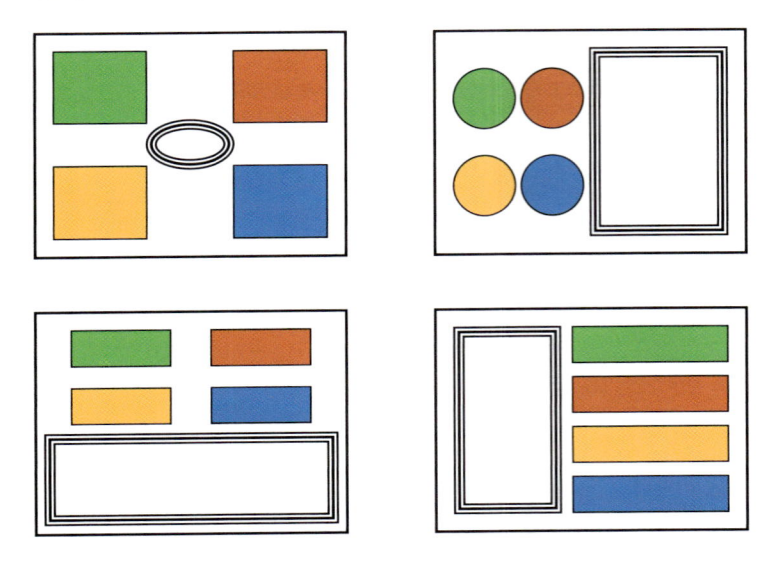

Hyperlinks

Hyperlinks are ways of linking web pages. The most common hyperlinks are created by using either text (**hypertext**) or images. By clicking on the word or image you are taken to another page with more information.

The diagram below shows how the character description and information web pages for one of the characters could be linked to the home page. The other character web pages could be linked in the same way.

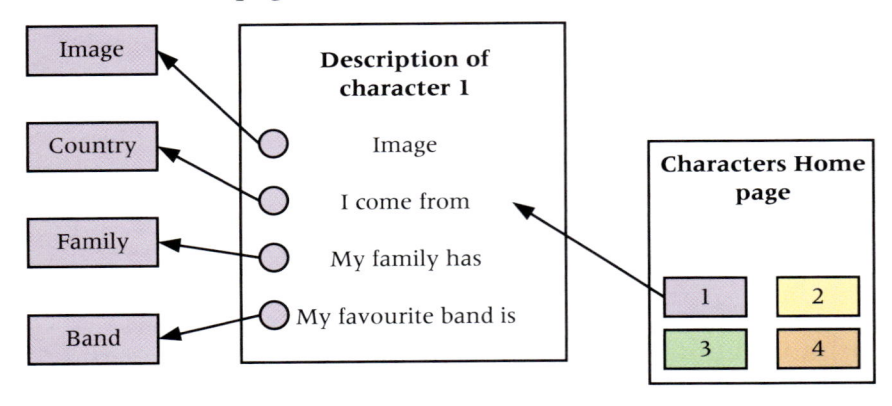

▶ *Skills help*

Using hyperlinks, page 63.

46

Unit 2.3

Module Task

Look again at the table you created in Task 1. Working with a partner decide which items of information will be on the home page of your web game and which will be on other pages. Enter the page you would like the information to go on in the final, unused column of the table. Also list the links you need for moving between the pages and back to the home page.

Resource 2.3 Web items will help you to make sure you have thought of everything.

Make sure that you have listed:
- text items
- images
- ways for moving between pages and back to the home page.

▶ Skills help

Navigating between web pages, page 63.

Hierarchical diagrams

A **hierarchical** tree diagram shows how the files are linked together, and all stored in one website folder.

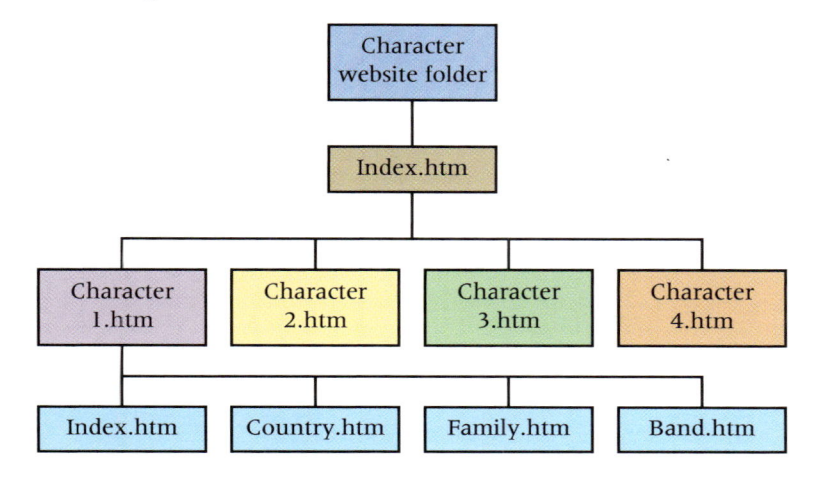

Task 2

Use quick, sketch diagrams like this to experiment with how your website might be laid out. When you have decided how you want your website to work, make a clear and accurate drawing of its hierarchical diagram.

47

Unit 2.3

Task 3

1. *Pull together all your facts in a table like the one below. Group together all the fact items for each web page, and group together all the web pages for each character.*

   List each item's type, for example text, image or hyperlink, the file that contains or will contain it, and check each item off when you have saved it in its file.

Item	Type	File name	Web page	Done it
Name	text	character1.htm	Character1	✓
Age	text	character1.htm	Character1	✓
etc			Character1	
Image of character	image	image1.htm	Character1	
Character1 image to country1 page	hyperlink		Character1	

2. *Invent descriptions and find the facts that you still need. Create or locate any missing images and store the image files in the **Character Website** folder. Tick the Done it column when you have the items ready for use in your web pages.*

Test centre

1. **What is a hyperlink?**
2. **What does navigating a web site mean?**
3. **What is a hierarchical tree diagram?**

Unit 2.4
Planning the structure of a web page

In this unit you are going to plan and create the layout for all the character web pages. You will learn how to add images and position them on a web page, so that they can be viewed in different web browsers.

Home page layout

What is usually found on a home page?

Most web pages have:

- Text areas
- Images
- Buttons to navigate the web pages

Where these features appear on the page depends upon the designer and the way that he/she has created the web page. Using HTML makes it hard to place items anywhere on the page, because it only allows items to be aligned left, centred or aligned right.

The best way to control the layout of a website so that it looks the same in different browsers, is to use a table to hold the different items. Here is a web page designed using a table that has seven rows and seven columns.

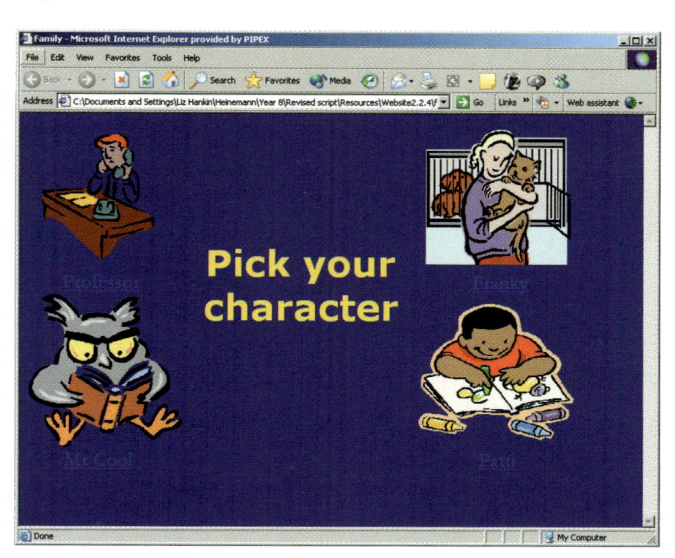

49

Here is the same website with the table visible.

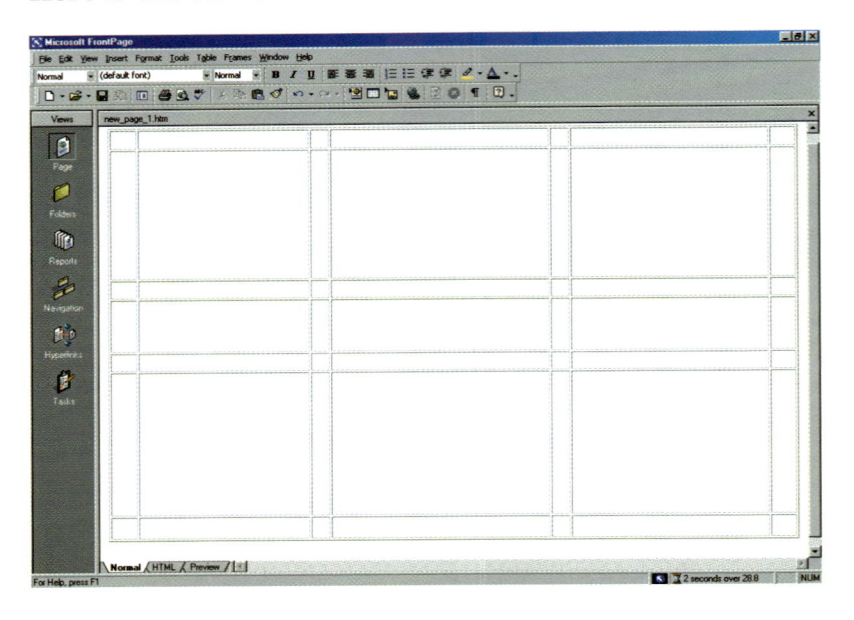

You can see where the width and height of columns and rows have been changed so items are displayed where the designer wants them to be.

In this case some of the cells in the columns and rows of the table are used as spaces. Alternatively you can change the cell spacing to set up a 3 × 3 cell table, with spaces between the cells, to do the same job.

▶ Skills help

Creating and formatting tables, pages 63–65.

Resource 2.4 Tables.

Using web design software

Web design software automatically sets up a new web page when the application is opened. It gives information about the web page as it is being created. You can see information about:

Task 1

To work out a suitable layout for your home page you are going to set up a sample web page using a word processing program.

1. Sketch out on paper where you would like the different items to appear on the home page.

2. Now work out how many columns and how many rows you need to make the table store all the items on the page.

3. Open a word processing program and create a table with the right number of rows and columns.

4. Save the file as Tables.htm.

5. Use the fact list you created in Task 3 of Unit 2.3 to help you place the items of information in the cells of the table.

6. Does the layout work? Do you need any extra rows or columns?

8. Make any changes that are needed to your table and save the file.

Common toolbar icons like those from Word

Download time

Tables can be created in the same way as in word processing software. Each cell in the table can be set up so that the contents are displayed as the designer wants. Images can be placed in the cells and the colours, fonts and alignment can all be changed. Cells can also be merged or split to adjust the position of items in the table.

▶ **Skills help**

Using web design software, pages 66–69.

Module Task

Remember that all of the web pages, images and graphics that you use in your website need to be stored in the **Character Website** *folder you created in Unit 2.1.*

1. *Create a new folder in your area of the school network. This will be used to store all of the web pages, images and graphics that you use in your website.*
2. *Open a web design program.*
3. *Use this program to create a home page with a table the same as you created in Task 1.*
4. *Use the fact list you created in Task 3 of Unit 2.3 to help you place the required items into their cells of the table.*
5. *Save the file as* **Index.htm** *in the* **Character Website** *folder you created in step 1. Remember* **index.htm** *is the Characters home page.*
6. *Add hyperlinks from the text, where the user can click to go to other pages about the characters.*
7. *Save and close your file again.*

▶ **Skills help**

Creating hyperlinks, pages 70–71.

Style sheets

To use the same colours, fonts and font styles on a series of web pages a **style sheet** can be used. HTML coding is used to instruct the computer to apply a set style to a web page.

The style sheet file extension is .css, which stands for **c**ascading **s**tyle **s**heet. It sets things like background colour, the font style and size, and the colour of hyperlinks as the mouse goes over them. It can also be set up so that the web page size can be viewed with any Internet browser.

Unit 2.4

Style sheets are useful because:
- they let a designer use the same style for all web pages without having to write lots of code
- the style can easily be changed for special users, for example to make it easier to read.

Task 2

Open **Resource 2.4 Family** in a web design program.

1. Look at the **HTML view** and find the line
   ```
   <link href="blue.css"
   type="text/css"
   rel="stylesheet">
   ```

2. Change the "blue.css" to "green.css" and look at the sheet in **Normal** and **Preview** view.

3. Describe what has happened.

4. Open Resource **2.4 Green style sheet** and see if you can work out why it has changed.

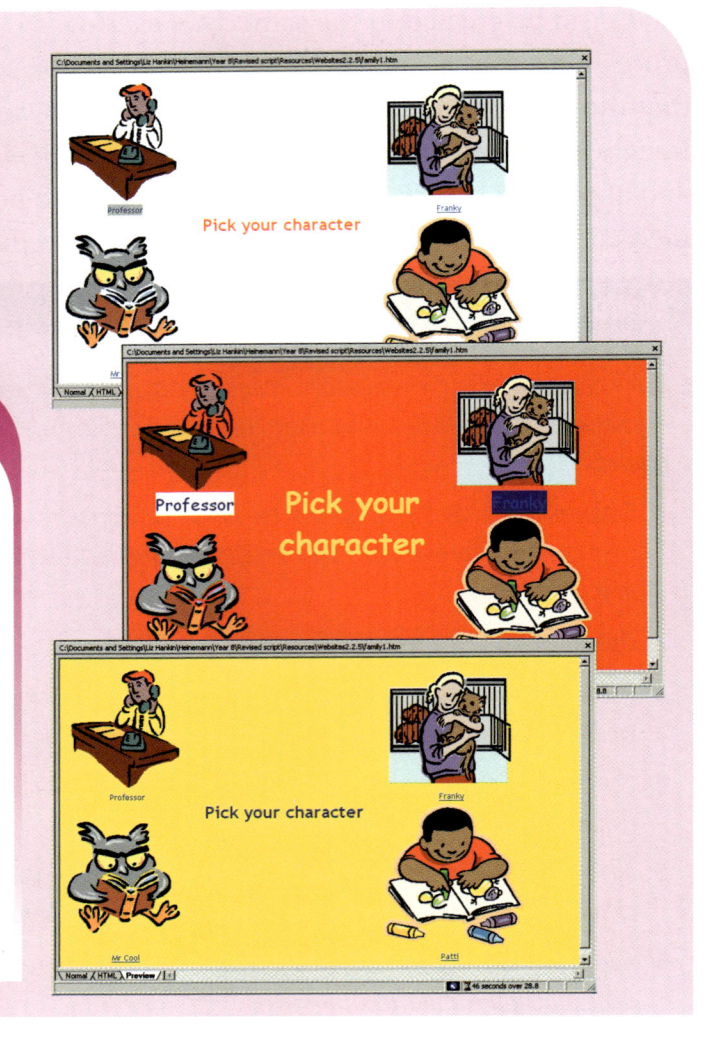

Task 3

In the next unit you are going to complete the web pages for all of the characters.

Make sure you have your fact list from Unit 2.3 to hand.

1. Take one of your characters and plan out the tables for all of the pages related to this character. When you are happy with them, do the same for the other three characters. You will probably want to use the same layouts for each type of page for all four characters, but obviously the content will be different for each one.

2. Before the next lesson locate all of the items of information and images that you still need.

Test centre

1. What is a home page?
2. Why do web designers use tables for creating web pages?
3. What is a style sheet?

Unit 2.5
Designing and creating a web page

In this unit you are going to create the remaining web pages for the characters and make sure that the navigation of the website works in the way that you intended.

'I always think that style is important'

Setting the style

The use of style sheets means that each web page will be set up to be displayed in the same way. However this does not mean that they will all look exactly the same. The font colours, styles and sizes can be set, but extra items can be added to a web page that has a style sheet in use. For example you might want to add the sound of an instrument to each web page, but you wouldn't want to add the same sound to each page, if each page is about a different instrument.

Task 1

Before creating the information pages about the characters you are going to select the style that you want to use for the whole of the website.

1. Open a web design program.
2. Copy folder **Resource 2.5 Style** and rename it. Find the file blue.htm in the folder and open it in the web design program.
3. In **Normal View**, type a heading and then set up a table on the web page and enter some text.
4. From the same folder, open each of these other sample files in turn:
   - Green.htm
   - White.htm
   - Red.htm
   - Yellow.htm

   Enter the same heading and table on each page.
5. What are the differences between the styles?
6. Choose one of these styles to be the basis for your web pages.

Remember – you can still add different things to different web pages if necessary.

53

Unit 2.5

Editing style sheets

If you like some of the features of a style sheet, but would like to change part of it, you can edit the file. To edit a style sheet you need to know how it is set up.

This is a copy of the **Resource 2.5 Blue style sheet**.

```
BODY    {font-family: Verdana,sans-serif;
         color: white; font-size: 18pt;
         background-color: navy}

TD      {font-family: Verdana,sans-serif;
         color: yellow; font-size: 14pt;
         background-color: navy}

H1      {font-size: 36pt}
H2      {font-size: 28pt}
H3      {font-size: 24pt}

A:hover {color: red; background-color: navy;
text-decoration: none; font-family:
Garamond; font-size: 20pt}

A:link {color: blue; background-color: navy;
font-family: Garamond; font-size: 20pt}

A:visited {color: navy; background-color:
white; text-decoration: none; font-family:
Garamond; font-size: 20pt}
```

Task 2

1. Open a web design application.
2. Open one of the .css files from your copy of the **Resource 2.5 Style** folder.
3. Experiment with editing the file and save it as a new .css file **in the same folder**.
4. Open the web page file, blue.htm *from the folder*.
5. Display the HTML code and find the line:

   ```
   <link rel="stylesheet" type="text/css" href="blue.css">
   ```

   Change "blue.css" to the new .css file that you have created.
6. Change to **Normal view** and add some text.
7. Does it look like you thought it would?

▶ *Skills help*

Using and editing style sheets, page 69.

Unit 2.5

Module Task

Having chosen a style sheet for the web pages you are ready to create the different pages for your characters.

1. Open the web page file that uses your chosen style sheet. Re-create your Character1 web page in this file.
2. Save it as **Character1.htm** in your **Character Website** folder. Create all the pages for character 1 before going on to the others.
3. Remember – save **all** web pages and images in your **Character Website** folder.
4. When you have created all the web pages, look at the hierarchical diagram for your website that you created in Unit 2.3, and create the hyperlinks between the pages.

▶ Skills help

Creating hyperlinks, pages 68–69.

> When you save files, give them names that mean something to you, this is important as you will use the file name to create the hyperlinks between the pages.

Site map

Users of websites sometimes want to know what is available on the website without having to navigate all the way around it.

Many websites have what is called a site map, this shows the structure of the website in an easy to read way. A site map is a simple version of a hierarchical tree diagram – the web pages are listed and there is a hyperlink to the web page from the diagram.

This is how a site map for the character website might look.

> You could use a site map to check that you have created all the files that you need for your website, and that they are all stored in the same folder.

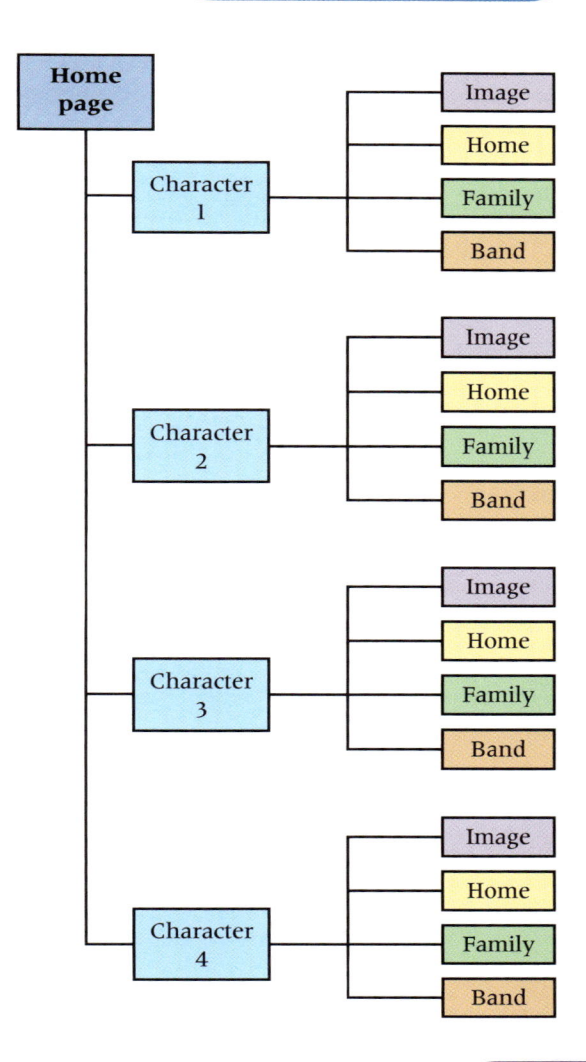

Home page
- Character 1
  - Image
  - Home
  - Family
  - Band
- Character 2
  - Image
  - Home
  - Family
  - Band
- Character 3
  - Image
  - Home
  - Family
  - Band
- Character 4
  - Image
  - Home
  - Family
  - Band

Task 3

1. Draw a site map for your character website.
2. Give a copy of the site map and access to your character website to another pupil. Ask them to use the map when they look at the website.

   Ask them to comment on:
   - how easy it is to use
   - if the language is correct
   - if the information is useful
   - if the images are clear and interesting.

Test centre

1. Why do web designers use style sheets?
2. What is a site map?
3. Why does all the content of the web pages have to be stored in the same folder?

Unit 2.6
Evaluating a website

In this unit you are going to evaluate the website that you have created and plan how it could be extended for a wider audience.

So does it work?

Websites are created for different reasons. Some are designed to sell things, or as a source of information, while others are for entertainment.

A website can be made to match its purpose by the way it looks and works, as well as the content it contains. Your website should be presenting information in an interesting way.

Before you go on to create the website game in Module 5 you need to make sure that you have got the right layout and navigation for the user.

To make sure that other people are happy with the website, they need to evaluate it against set criteria. There are three aspects to the evaluation:

- the design of the website
- the structure of the website
- the quality of the information.

Unit 2.6

Task 1

Open **Resource 2.6 Evaluation criteria** and **Resource 2.6 Evaluation form**.

1. Make a list of four criteria under each of the three headings given below that users will be able to use to evaluate your website. For example:

Design	Structure	Quality
• Layout is clear, with a balance of space and items	• There is an easy way to navigate around the website	• The information is relevant
•	•	•

2. Create an evaluation form based on these criteria that other people in your class can complete when they use your website.

Planning ahead

When the navigation of a website is planned it needs to take into account that the website might be expanded at a later date and more pages added. The website might also be used in different ways in the future.

For your web game you need to plan the navigation so that it matches the original request.

PLEASE HELP!

We need an interesting section on the community website that will make people of your age want to look at the website.

We want a simple game that users could have fun with and that show links between our community and four other countries that we have links with:

- Australia
- Canada
- France
- Singapore

Task 2

1. Create a list of all the items you will need to gather together for the new web pages.

2. Create a new folder in your area of the school network. This will be used to store all the web pages and images that you use in your website. Call this folder **Web game website XX and YY** (XX and YY should be your initials and your partners initials.

3. Copy or move the **Character Website** folder into this folder ready for later work.

Unit 2.6

So to plan ahead for the game you need to work out how to set up the navigation for these areas:

- Community website home page and the 'Young peoples' section.
- 'Young peoples' section home page to the character website home page.
- 'Young peoples' section home page to the four countries' web pages.
- The countries' web pages to other web pages that hold information on:
  – up to date information about the music charts in the four countries
  – information about how schools are set up in the four countries
  – information about the best methods of travel to these countries.

Module Task

Work with a partner to plan out the young people's section of the website.

Use the methods that you have learnt within this Module to show how the web pages displaying these four areas of information could be linked together - don't worry about the layout of these pages, that will happen when you put the game together, just make sure that you have a structure and a navigation route planned.

▶ Skills help

Navigating between web pages, page 63.

Resource Specification.

Test centre

1. Give three aspects of a website that could be used in its evaluation?
2. What methods can be used to 'navigate' a website on screen?
3. What could happen to the navigation of a website if extra pages are added?

59

Module 2 — Assignment

Web pages

To complete Module 2 you are going to produce a two page website providing information about one of the countries that a character in your web game comes from.

This is a sample of web page for you to copy.

Using a web page design method that you know about, produce your own version of this web page. Alternatively you could create your own style and layout for the web page.

Images are available from the Image Bank on the network.

Produce a second page that looks like this one.

Create hyperlinks between these two pages.

Save your web pages with suitable names.

Evaluate your web pages and make notes about how you could improve them.

- Think about the ways you created web pages in this module and select the way that suits you best:
  - HTML
  - word processed and saved as *.htm* file
  - with a web design program.
- Think about how a user will move between these two pages.

Module 2 — Skills help

Using HTML

Tags
Code items are known as tags.

A tag starts and ends with `<` and `/>` symbols. There are start tags, like `<body>` and end tags, like `</body>`. Tags like these mark the beginning and end of a section of web page coding.

Start tags like `<b>` turn on an effect, in this case bold, whilst the end tag `</b>` turns off the effect.

`<html>` `</html>`
Is used to start and end the coding

`<head>` `</head>`
Is used at the head and end of a page

`<title>` `</title>`
Is used at the beginning and end of a title

`<body>` `</body>`
Is used at the beginning and end of the main content of the page

`<h1 align=center>` `</h1>`
Is used to set up and end the alignment of a heading

`<br>`
This puts the text that comes after it on a new line. Try it with your *description1.htm* file. There is no end tag for line break.

If you want to space the lines further, put in extra `<br>`s. For example `<br><br>` will give a line break and one extra line of space.

`<p>` `</p>`
Is used to create a paragraph on a web page and is used along with alignment coding, the same as with headings. For example:

Paragraph, align text left
`<p align=left></p>`

Paragraph, text centred
`<p align=center></p>`

Paragraph, align text right
`<p align=right></p>`

Paragraph, justify text
`<p align=justify></p>`

A paragraph tab puts a line break after itself.

The code will work without the `</p>` tag, but it is best to use it.

Fonts and styles
Different fonts can be selected using
`<font face="****"></font>`.

Replace the "*****" with the font name, for example:
`<font face="arial"></font>`
would display the text in Arial font.

Font colours
`<font color="***"></font>`
Is used to display fonts in different colours.

`<font color="red"></font>`
Would display the font in red.

Colours available are: white, black, grey, silver, red, maroon, fuchsia, purple, green, lime, teal, olive, blue, aqua, navy and yellow.

Font styles
`<b></b>` makes the text bold.
`<i></i>` is used for italics.

Background colour
`<bgcolor="******">`
Is used to set the background colour by adding to the 'body' tag.

`<body bgcolor="silver">`
Would turn the background into a light grey colour.

Skills 2

Selecting different formats of files when you save

1 Go to **File**.
2 Select **Save As**. The following dialogue box appears.

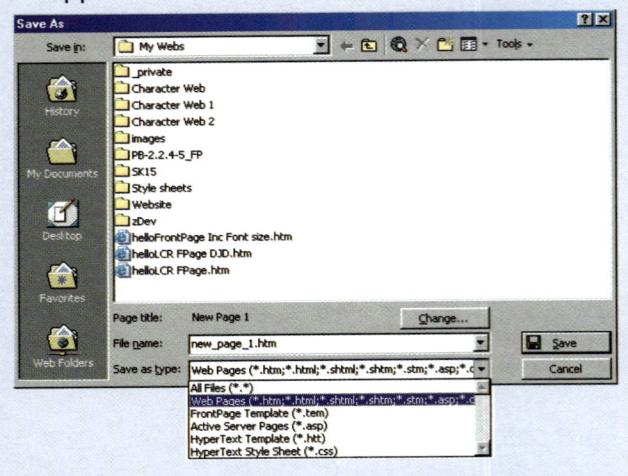

3 Click on the arrow at the end of the **Save as type** box.

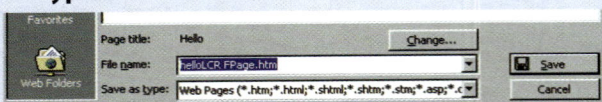

4 Select **Web Page (*.htm;*.html)**.

Your filename will now have an *.htm* extension and you will be able to open it in a web browser like Internet Explorer.

Finding out the size of files

In Windows Explorer open the folder containing the following two web page files – **Resource 2 Web page Word** and **Resource 2 Web page Notepad**.

The file sizes, 1KB and 3KB are shown.

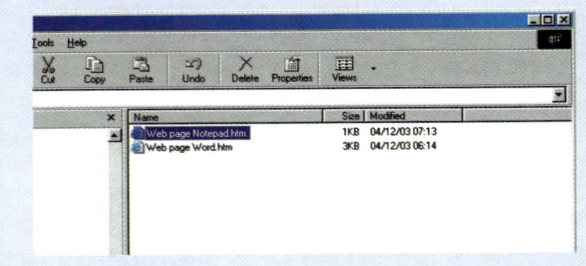

A more accurate file size is displayed in the bottom bar of Windows Explorer.

Properties

More information can be seen by looking at the properties of a file.

1 Right click on the **Resource 2 Web Page Notepad** file.
2 Select and click on **Properties** in the menu.

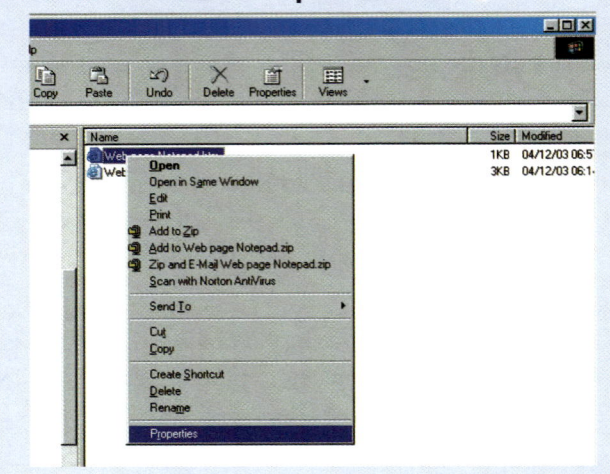

62

Although the file size is only 303 bytes, 16,384 bytes are used to store it on the hard drive.

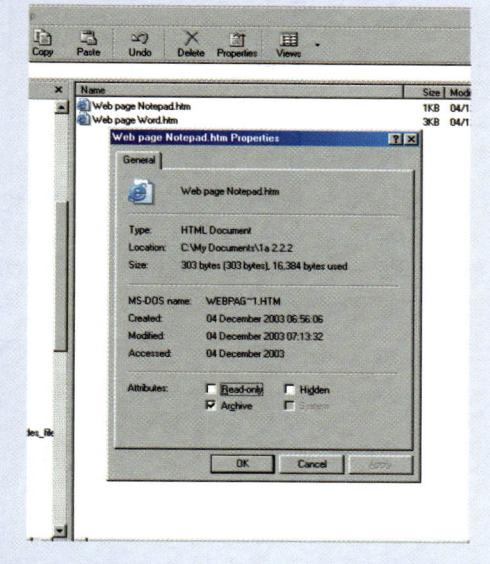

3 Do the same to see the properties of the web page file created in Word (**Resource 2 Web Page Word**).

It shows the size of this file is 3,014 bytes, and again 16,384 bytes are used to store the file.

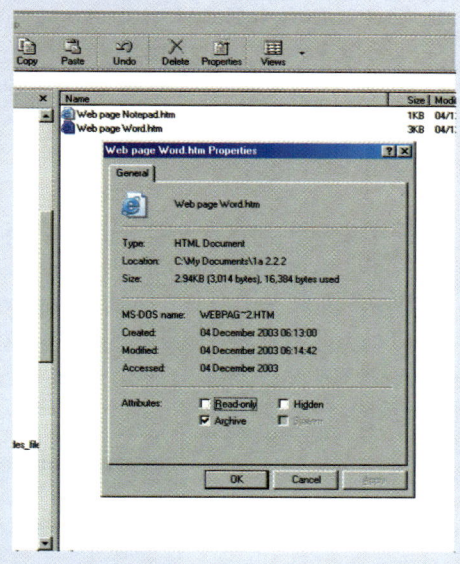

The web page created in Word is about 10 times bigger than the same web page created by writing the basic HTML code for the page in Notepad.

Although the computer uses up the same disc space to store the two files, the fact that files created in Notepad are so much smaller means that they will open faster over the Internet.

Using hyperlinks and navigating between web pages

Hyperlinks are used to move from one web page to another. Hyperlinks can be either:
- Hypertext, e.g. David's Page
- An image or graphic.

Web pages often have a line of hyperlinks. This is called a navigation bar, for example:

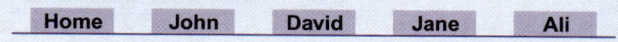

| Home | John | David | Jane | Ali |

In a web browser, such as Internet Explorer, clicking on a hyperlink takes you to a different page.

Clicking on the **Back** arrow takes you back to the last page visited.

In a word processor, the Back arrow in the Web toolbar becomes active.
Clicking this takes you back.

Tables

Creating and formatting tables
1 Click the cursor at the place you want the table to appear.
2 Select **Insert**, **Table** from the **Table** menu.

Skills 2

3 The following dialogue box will then appear.

4 Enter the number of rows and columns you need in the **Table size** boxes. This example sets up a 7 × 7 table.
5 Click **OK** and the table will appear.

Setting the alignment of the table
1 Right mouse click anywhere inside the table and select **Table Properties**.

2 Click the **Options** button in the **Table Properties** dialogue box and uncheck the **Automatically resize to fit contents** checkbox.
3 Look at **Default cell margins** and change them if you need to.
4 Click **OK**

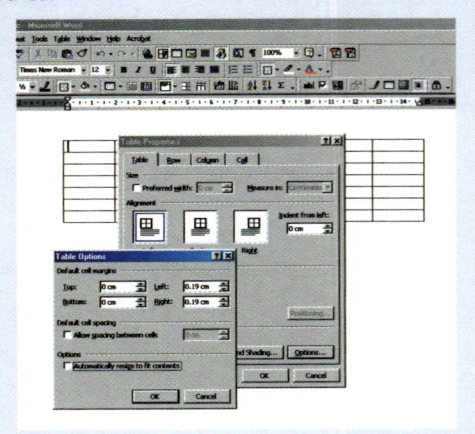

5 In the **Table properties** dialogue box click the **Center** icon in **Alignment**. This centres the data in the cells.
6 Click **OK** again.

Setting the height of rows
1 Place the cursor in the second row of your table.
2 Right mouse click and open **Table Properties** again.
3 Click the **Row** tab and tick the **Specify height** checkbox.

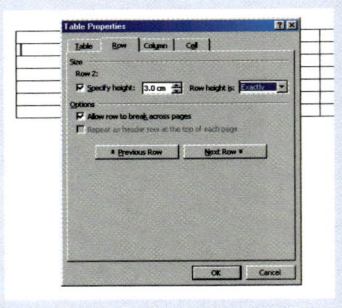

4 Enter the height you want for the second row.
5 Select **Exactly** from the drop down list in the **Row height is** box.
6 Click the **Next Row** button twice and set the height for the fourth row in the same way.
7 Again click the **Next Row** button twice and set the height for the sixth row.
8 Click **OK**.

Setting the width of columns
1 Click the cursor in the first column.
2 Right click and select **Table Properties**.
3 Click the **Column tab** and enter the width you want for your first column in the **Preferred width** box.

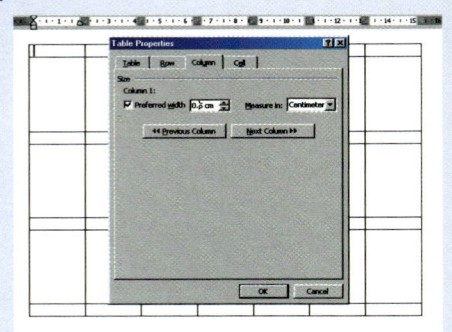

64

4 Click the **Next Column** button and set the width for the second column in the same way.
5 Repeat this until you have set all the column widths as you want them.
6 Click **OK**.

Using cell spacing

Rather than using blank columns and rows to separate the content in a web page, you can achieve the same layout using cell spacing and cell margins to separate cell content.

1 Click the **Insert Table** icon in the toolbar and select a 3 × 3 table.

2 Right mouse click on the table and select **Table Properties**.
3 Select **Options** from the **Table properties** dialogue box.
4 Check the **Allow spacing between cells** box and set the spacing to 0.5cm.
5 Uncheck the **Automatically resize to fit contents** box.
6 Look at the **Default cell margins** and change them if you need to.
7 Click **OK**.

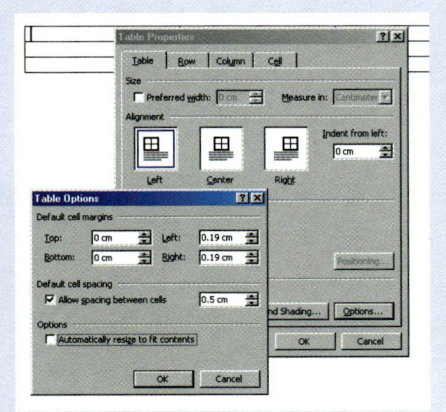

8 Select the **Center** icon in **Alignment**.
9 Click **OK** again.

Borders

It is possible to hide the borders so they do not show on the web page.

1 Right click in the table and select **Borders and Shading**
or
Click the **Borders and Shading** button in the **Table Properties** dialogue box.
2 Click the **None** icon in **Setting**.

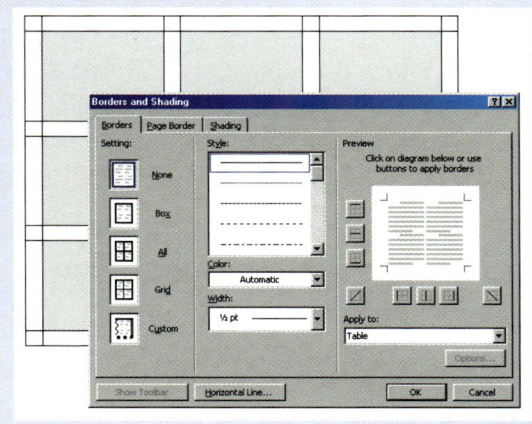

3 Click **OK**.

Adding rows

1 Click in a cell where the row is to be added above or below.
2 Select **Insert**, **Rows Below** or **Rows Above** from the **Table** menu.

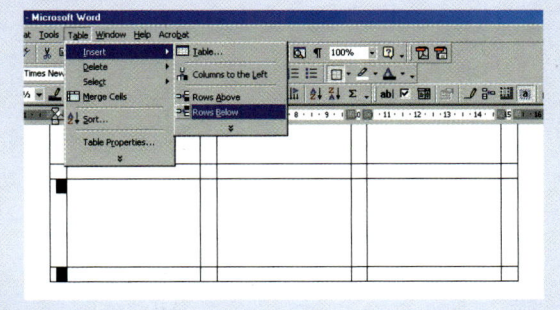

Columns can be added from the same menu, but it is best to add them one at a time.

Skills 2

Using web design software

FrontPage is a web design program that has word processing tools and can be used in much the same way as MS Word.

FrontPage opens with a new page.

Click on **File** in the menu bar and select **Save As** to store all the web pages, images and graphics that will be used in a website.

Different view in FrontPage

At the bottom of the screen you can see three tabs. These tabs allow you to look at the web page being created in:

- Normal view – like a word processor view and where you can do most of the design work.
- HTML view – showing the coding.
- Preview view – shows you how it will appear on the internet as a web page.

Tools

The tools for setting up the colours and fonts are the same ones as found within MS Word.

Select **Format** from the menu bar.

The different items in the menu can be used to select:

- font type, style and colour
- background colour
- a theme for the whole website.

This shows the **Font** dialogue box.

Using tables to create web page layout

1. Click **Table** from the menu bar and select **Insert**.

2. Set the number of rows and columns that you want in the table.
3. Right mouse click on the table to open **Table Properties**.

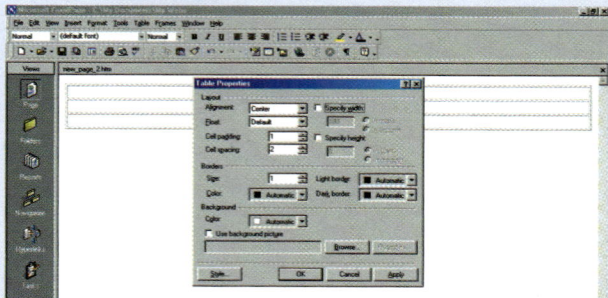

66

Table Properties in FrontPage is like the Table Properties in Word. Although instead of **Cell margins** there is something called **Cell padding**.

Cell spacing is the same as it is in Word, but is not set up in centimetres.

If you leave the **Specify width** box unchecked, then the cells in the table grow in size as you enter text into them like this.

Typing in a cell causes the table to resize in quite an unpredictable way.

4 Set the **Layout Alignment** to **Centre**.
5 Check the **Specify height box** and set the height to 100%, the default setting.
6 Set **Cell padding** to 4 and **Cell spacing** to 20.

This will allow the table to work in whatever size window someone is using to look at the web page.

Click the **HTML** tab to see the code that creates this table.

Changing the size of cells in the table to change the layout on the web page

1 Select all the cells and right mouse click on the table.
2 The **Cell Properties** dialogue box is opened.

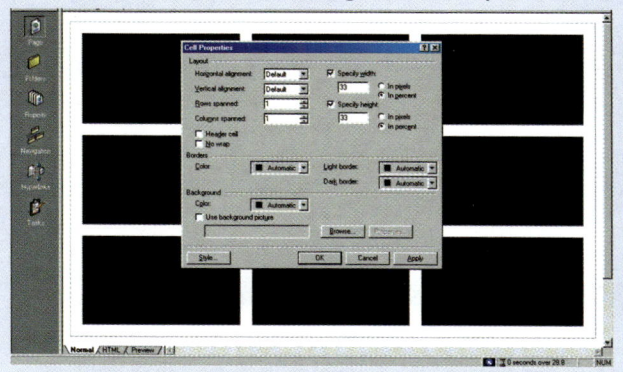

3 Change the **Specify width** and **Specify height** values (here it has been changed to 33%) to alter the proportions of the cells in the table.
4 Make sure the default for text wrapping is shown.

The table will look like this one.

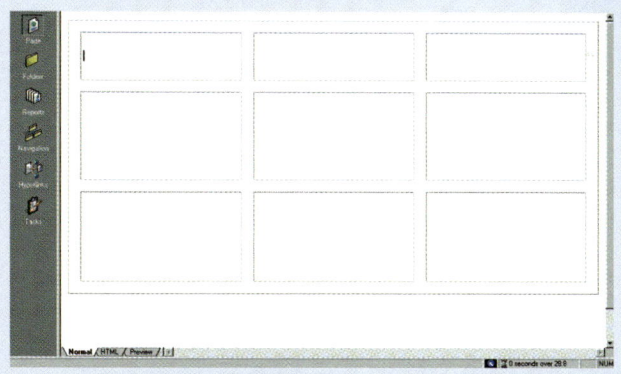

Merging cells in the table

1 Select two cells next to each other.
2 Right mouse click, and select **Merge Cells**.

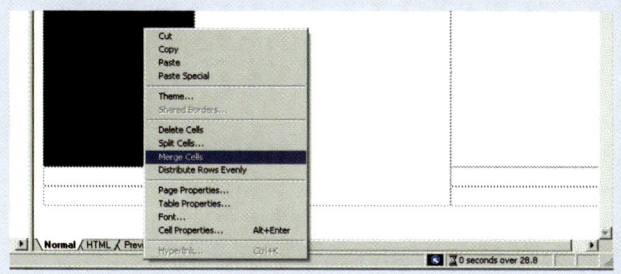

67

Skills 2

By merging cells the layout of the table can be changed very easily.

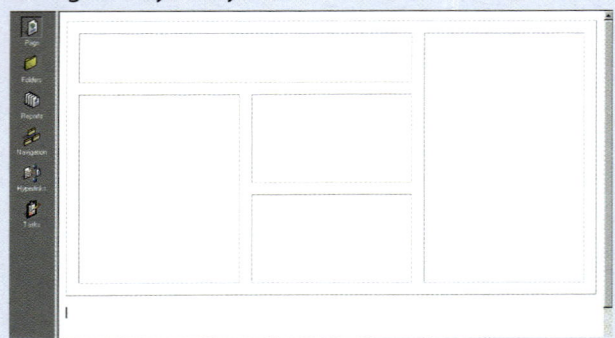

Adding items to the table
1. Select **Normal View** from the **View** menu.
2. Click in the cell of the table where you want to enter some text or an image.
3. Add the items in the same way as you would in a table in Word.

Using hypertext for hyperlinks
Hyperlinks allow you to click on words or images to move to another web page or website.

For this to work there will need to be web page file to move to, stored either in the same folder or as another website. The web pages themselves do not need to be created yet, just a file saved ready.

Creating your empty web pages in a folder for a hyperlink
1. Click on **File** and select **New**.
2. Go to **Save As** and type in one of your character's names. Make sure that it is saving the file in the right folder (the one where the home page is saved).
3. Now do the same for all the other links that are to be created.

There should now be the home page file and all the character page files in the same folder.

Creating the hyperlinks
1. Open your home page file in **Normal View** in FrontPage.
2. Highlight the name of one of the characters.
3. Click **Insert** in the menu bar and select **Hyperlink**. 
4. Select the web page file for the character from the website folder and click **OK**.

68

5 Save the file.
6 Now do the same for the other characters.
7 Save the file.

Previewing the hyperlinks

1 Open the home page in **Normal View**.
2 Click on the **Preview** tab at the bottom of the page.

3 Click on any of the character names and it should take you to the empty character page that you have prepared ready for developing.
4 Click on the **Normal** tab at the bottom of the page to return to your home page file.

Hiding cell borders

1 In **Normal View** right mouse click in a cell in your table.
2 Select **Table properties** and set the **Borders Size** to 0.

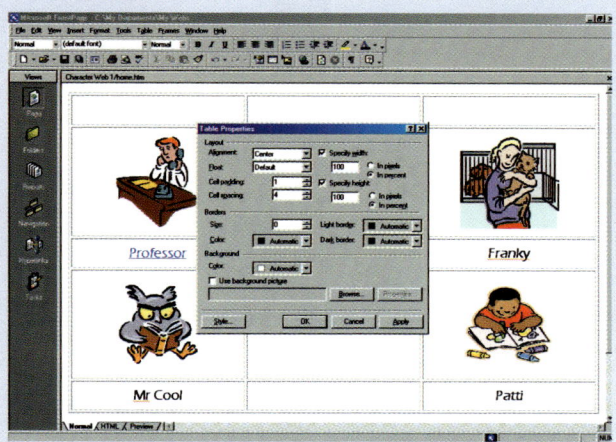

The borders now appear as dotted lines in **Normal View** but disappear in **Preview**.
3 Save your file.

Using and editing style sheets

To change the font and background colour of a website, the code in the first line of the style sheet would have to be changed.

`BODY {font-family:` **`Verdana,sans-serif;`** `color: white; font-size: 18pt; background-color:` **`navy`**`}`

is changed to

`BODY {font-family:` **`Arial;`** `color: white; font-size: 18pt; background-color:` **`plum`**`}`

This new version will display the text in Arial font with a plum coloured background.
Other lines in the style sheet can be edited in the same way.

Changing website appearance

Turning off fonts and font styles

1 Go to **Tools** and select **Internet Options**.
2 The **Internet Options** dialogue box will appear. Click on the **Accessibility** button.
3 Check the tick boxes to turn off the fonts and font styles
4 Click **OK**. Click **OK** again.

Turning off graphics

1 Go to **Tools** and select **Internet options**.
2 The **Internet Options** dialogue box will appear. Click on the **Advanced** tab.
3 Scroll down the list until you reach **Multimedia**. Uncheck the **Show Pictures** tick box.
4 Click **Apply**, then click **OK**.
5 Click the refresh button and the webpage will appear without graphics.

Module 3
Information – reliability, validity and bias

Learning Targets

During this module you are going to find out about the best methods of locating reliable information.

As part of the development of your web game you need to find out accurate and reliable information about life for people of your age in four countries. These countries are:
- Australia
- France
- Canada
- Singapore

You will also create a database to store some information that is given to you and have a chance to use a relational database.

In Module 3 you are going to learn:

How to evaluate information given to you from unknown sources	See pages 74–76
How to identify what is a fact and what is an opinion	See pages 74–75
How to evaluate which information is useful for different tasks	See page 76
About copyright laws and how they affect you	See pages 77–78
How to use a wide range of search techniques, such as AND, OR and NOT	See pages 79–81
How to evaluate and use full text searches	See page 81
How to create a database for storing and retrieving information	See page 83–84
How to use a relational database to produce simple reports	See pages 89–90
About data protection	See pages 91–94

Learning Targets 3

What are your targets for this module?

To achieve a level 4 in this module you will need to
- Demonstrate why you need to know the difference between fact and opinion
- Understand the best ways to find out if information is suitable to use for completing specific tasks
- Use a range of search techniques on the Internet and computer systems to find information that you need, including the use of AND, OR and NOT
- Understand that there are restrictions on the use of information and images because of copyright laws
- Create a simple database to store given data
- See how a relational database is different from a flat file database in how it stores information
- Use a range of search techniques to find information from your database
- Produce simple reports from your database
- Find out how personal data can be protected by organisations and individuals

To achieve a level 5 in this module you will need to
- Demonstrate how you tell the difference between fact and opinion
- Evaluate the relevance of information for completing specific tasks
- Use a range of appropriate search techniques to locate information from the Internet and other computerised databases
- Demonstrate knowledge about copyright law and how it can affect the use of information and images in your work
- Create a database to store given data and use a range of techniques to search the database for information
- Know the differences between a flat file database and a relational database, and say which would be most effective for different purposes
- Combine the use of different software products to produce some reports showing information you have found from your database
- Discuss the law relating to the storing of personal data and its implications for organisations that hold data about people

To achieve a level 6 in this module you will need to
- Analyse information to determine whether it is fact or opinion
- Evaluate the accuracy, reliability and validity of data for completing specific tasks and be able to make recommendations to others
- Choose and use efficiently a range of advanced search techniques to locate information from the Internet and other computerised databases
- As a matter of course, take into account copyright issues when using information and images
- Construct, test and document the development of a relational database. You should produce a design specification and think about appropriate ways of inputting and validating the data
- Carry out queries and searches on your database using the most effective methods for each task
- Discuss the structure of a relational database and show how data is dealt with more efficiently than in a flat file database
- Use a relational database to produce reports for a specific purpose
- Discuss the use and misuse of personal data in a range of contexts

Learning Targets 3

What do you know already?

Using spreadsheet software

A spreadsheet is like a **table** drawn out on the computer screen. The table is made up of cells. The cells are in rows and columns. To be able to identify a single cell, they are each given a **cell reference**. The rows and columns all have labels.

Table. A table is made up of rows and columns of cells, which can contain text and/or numbers. Generally the columns are fields, and the rows are records.

Cell reference. This tells you where a cell is, using the column letters and row numbers, e.g. A1.

Flat file database

A database set up in a spreadsheet such as MS Excel is a flat file database. The data for each **record** is keyed in, and if any changes to the data are needed each separate record has to be edited.

Record. A record is a collection of related data divided into separate elements. For example, the record for an address would have separate elements for house number, road, town and postcode. The house number, road and town are **fields**.

Field. A field is an individual element within a record.

Relational database

A relational database is made up of a series of data tables, each table contains some information that relates to a field in a record. If data changes then only the data in the table has to be changed as the record is then updated.

Data types

Different data types are used so that calculations, searches and sorts on data can be done efficiently. The two main types of data are **alphanumeric** and **numeric**.

Alphanumeric. Alphanumeric data can be a mixture of numbers and text. A postcode is alphanumeric.

Numeric. Numeric data is limited to numbers only and can be formatted in different ways, for example as a **percentage** (%).

Percentage. A percentage shows a value for numeric data. It is often used when numbers need to be compared.

Sorting data

Data can be sorted in a variety of different ways, for example **filtering**.

Filtering. Filtering allows you to just see the data you want – it filters out unwanted data. You can set conditions for sorts, for example AND/OR.

Searching for information

A search can be carried out to find documents, words or information. The searches that are used in these tasks are **text searches**, and **AND OR and NOT** searches.

Text searches. Text searches are used to locate text in documents or websites. Text searches can be set up to find whole words or parts of words.

AND, OR and NOT. Searches sometimes need to find more than one item of information, or information that has more than one way of being identified, for example:
It is red AND square
It is red AND square but NOT shiny
It is red AND square OR shiny

Learning Targets 3

Task

The words below and their meanings have been jumbled up.
Can you match each word to its correct meaning?

Relational database	An individual item of data within a record
Alphanumeric	Finds information that contains one word but not another
AND search	Tells you where a cell is using column letter and row number
Record	Putting data in a particular order
NOT search	A series of data tables that are linked together
Table	A way of only showing data that matches specific criteria
Cell reference	Finds a particular word or part of a word
Text search	A collection of related items of data divided into fields
Field	Number data
Sorting	Finds information that contains one word or another
Numeric	Finds information that contains both words
Filtering	Contains rows and columns
OR search	A mixture of text and number data

73

Unit 3.1
Evaluating information

In this unit you will see how important it is to examine information carefully to see whether it is believable.

Do you believe it?

When you are presented with new information you have to decide whether it is reliable and plausible.

Information can either be a fact or an opinion. The use of words such as *think*, *seems*, *could* and *should*, can indicate an opinion. The table contains some information about London and Rome, some is fact, and some is opinion.

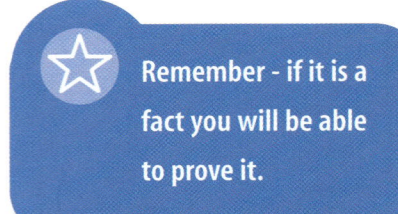

> Remember - if it is a fact you will be able to prove it.

London is in England	Fact	Yes it is and the fact can be proved
London is the largest city	Fact or opinion	It is the largest city in England, but not in the world
I think everyone loves London	Opinion	The word *think* lets you know that it is only somebody's opinion
Londoners should all be allowed to travel for free	Opinion	A lot of people might agree, but it is not a fact
London is a cleaner city than Rome	Fact or Opinion	This could be true but who has made the judgement? Does it mean the air, the streets, people's windows? One person might think something is clean whilst another does not
Rome is a long way from London	Fact or opinion	Where are you starting from? If you have travelled from South America to London, then Rome is not very far away, compared to how far you have already travelled. But if you live in Oxford, then Rome might seem a long way away, compared to London.

Unit 3.1

Task 1

1. Write down three facts about your school.
2. Write down three opinions about your school.
3. Read out your list to a partner and see if they can tell you which is fact and which is opinion.

Whose opinion is it?

Opinions can be worth taking notice of. Experts in a subject can make statements that give their own viewpoint, and sometimes it is not possible to prove that the information is true. However, because their opinion is based on their detailed knowledge of a subject, this opinion can be important.

> 'By the time a man realises that maybe his father was right, he usually has a son who thinks he's wrong.'
> Charles Wadsworth, Artistic Director and Chamber Musician

> 'There is no reason for any individual to have a computer in his home.'
> Kenneth H Olson, President of Convention of the World Future Society, 1977

Does Charles Wadsworth's opinion come from knowledge of a subject?

Kenneth H Olsen is an expert in the field of computers. If you had heard his **assumption** about the future of computers in 1977 would you have thought he was wrong?

When you look at websites you need to know who owns the website to see if a piece of information is a fact or an opinion, and whether the opinion is from an expert. The URL and domain type can tell you about who owns a website. For example, the domain *.gov* tells you that a website is owned by a government, so you can probably trust this information.

Task 2

You are going to look at some websites and work out who owns the sites, from their domain type.

The websites can be accessed by going to http://www.heinemann.co.uk/hotlinks

Open **Resource 3.1 Website owners**.

Complete the table by entering the URL against the owner. Add the matching domain type from the list below the table. One has been done for you.

Unit 3.1

So who should you believe?

If you wanted to find out information about courses at a university would you look at a *.org*, a *.com* or a *.ac* website? There are lots of clues that help you evaluate the value of a website.

You need to check:
- the reliability of the information on the website
- the suitability of the owner for providing information that is suitable for your task.

You also need to consider the source of the information.

If you wanted to find out the latest news about travelling to a country would you choose a CD, a software game or the Internet? Why is this?

If you wanted to find out about the mountain ranges in a country would you have to use the same source? Why?

What is the difference between these two situations?

Links

Websites often provide links to other sites that have similar content. However it is not possible for the owners of a website to control who creates links to their site.

Task 3

Open **Resource 3.1 Information sources**.

Think about the questions on the left. Use them to help you create a list of five criteria that you could use against sources of information, to make sure they are the best ones to use for a task. The first one has been done for you.

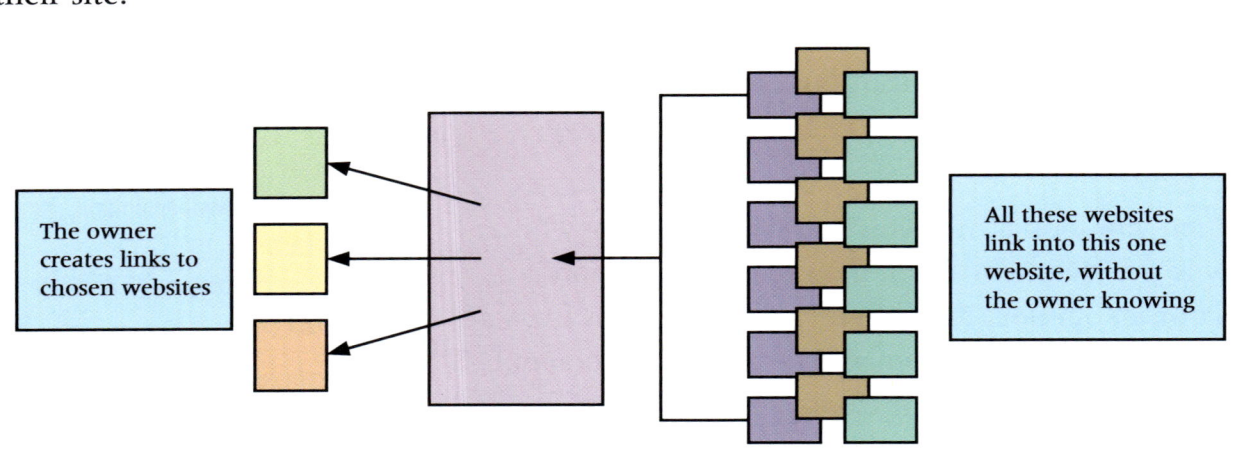

The owner creates links to chosen websites

All these websites link into this one website, without the owner knowing

76

This could be a good thing, because it means that lots of people find links to the website. But it could also mean that the site becomes linked to some undesirable websites.

> **Skills help**
>
> Bookmarking web pages, page 25 Module 1.

Module Task

To gather information for your web game you need to find out reliable information about the way people of your age are living in the four countries.

Look at the websites about Australia, Canada, France and Singapore, which can be accessed by going to:

http://www.heinemann.co.uk/hotlinks

1 Which of these websites do you think provides the most reliable information about the way of life in these countries? Why?

2 Do the websites contradict each other?

3 Complete **Resource 3.1 Websites** by stating why you believe the information on a website, or what reason you have for disbelieving it.

4 Bookmark the websites that you will use again to gather information for your web game.

Copyright

If somebody creates something that is 'fixed' in place, for example a written document, a picture, a film, or a website, then it is protected by copyright.

The copyright symbol © followed by a name and date warns others against copying it without getting permission first. If you are given permission to use any copyright material, you must always acknowledge the source of this material in your work.

The types of works that can be copyrighted are:
- literary works such as novels, instruction manuals, computer programs, song lyrics and newspaper articles
- dramatic works, including dance and mime
- musical works

Unit 3.1

- artistic works such as paintings, engravings, photographs, sculptures, collages, architectural drawings, technical drawings, diagrams, maps and logos
- sound recordings such as tapes, CDs and DVDs
- films, including videos and broadcasts.

But copyright does not protect the idea, it only protects the actual item. So someone could reproduce the same idea in their own way, without breaching the copyright laws.

Task 4

Open **Resource 3.1 My country fact file**.

Here are some things that are different in different countries:
- *capital city*
- *major towns or cities*
- *typical food*
- *school life (age you start/leave school, time school starts/finishes)*

To start your thinking on this, list facts about your own country and school life.

Facts like these will form the basis of the clues in your web game.

Test centre

1 What does *.gov* tell someone?
2 What criteria can you use to make sure you are using suitable information?
3 What can be protected by copyright?

Unit 3.2
Searching for information

In this unit you will learn how to carry out searches to obtain information effectively from the Internet and electronic sources. You will use conditional searches and refine the way in which you use search engines.

Searching questions

Using search engines to find information is easy, using search engines to find the information that you really need takes a bit more planning.

To help you find exactly what it is you are looking for you can add some words, called **Boolean connectors**, to your search, these are:

AND – Put AND in your search if you want to find information that contains both words, for example 'currency AND exchange rates'.

OR – Put OR in your search if you want to find information containing either one word or another, for example 'flights OR air travel'.

NOT – Put NOT in your search if you want to find information containing the first word, but not the second, for example 'football NOT American'.

Some search engines, such as Google, do not need AND to be entered between words, because it assumes that if more than one word has been typed in, they must be related to each other.

Using the NOT word

The use of **NOT** in a search can sometimes produce the same results as you would get if you used an AND search, but it can be used to eliminate some information from a list.

Task 1

Look at these shapes.

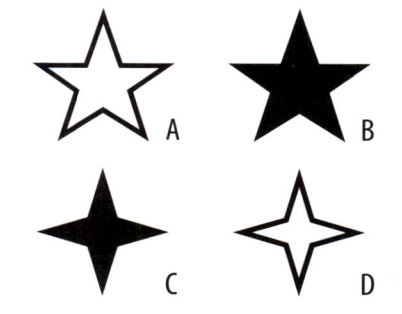

A ☆ B ★

C ◆ D ✦

1 Open **Resource 3.2 Stars** and complete the table by entering the letter or letters for the shapes that match the description.

2 Which description matches only one star?

79

Unit 3.2

For example the following descriptions match this star.

- This star is NOT black AND does NOT have 4 points.
- This star is white AND has 5 points.

I am NOT tall AND NOT blond AND NOT fat AND NOT thin AND I wear glasses OR NOT.

Tricks for searching

Using an accurate description of the information needed from a search may not always be enough. There are a number of other ways to refine your search.

Precise strings – You can search for a particular phrase or name using a precise string. Text searches can be set up to look for a set of letters or a complete word in documents.

Text searches can be asked to match the case of words, so that they find only words that began with capital letters, or words that sound like one another – really good for finding words like bow and bough.

Finding a set of letters can be useful when searching for text in long documents, but care has to be taken as it can also sometimes bring up strange combinations from words that come close to each other in a document.

▶ **Skills help**

Text searches in Word, page 96.

Task 2

Look at this list of words that have been found using a text search

Their	Other	With either
There	Gather	Either
These	With each	The

Which type of text search has been set up? Can you work out which letters were used in the search?

Computer system searches

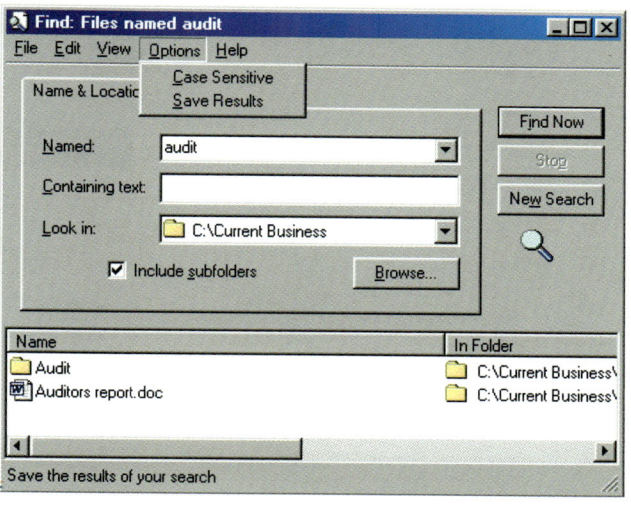

Searches can be carried out on the whole of a computer system (or network) to find specific words in files or folders. This is a powerful way of finding the information needed.

The search can find folders, files or documents that contain the key words in the search – just like a search engine on the Internet.

It is also possible to search for files or documents that were created or modified within set dates. So if all you can remember is when you worked on a file, then you can find it this way.

If you cannot remember what the file is called, but know what type it is, you can carry out something called a wild card search, this will look for every file that meets your wild card search. A symbol is used instead of letters or filenames, for example:

SA*.doc

This wild card search would find all Word files that have a filename beginning with SA.

Skills help

System searches, pages 96–97.

Search engines on the web

A good way to carry out effective searches is to write down a short description of exactly what it is you want to find out. This makes you concentrate on the content rather than the search. For example you could need to find:

The company that provides the cheapest air travel to Australia, which allows you to book online and also arranges for transfer to and from the airport.

The key words that you use in the search could be:

Cheap   **Air travel**   **Australia**

Unit 3.2

Module Task

For each of the four countries in the web game you need to find facts on the following items:
- capital city
- major towns and cities
- age children start school
- age children leave school
- typical food.

Open **Resource 3.2 Four countries fact file 1**.

1 Use the websites that you bookmarked earlier for finding facts on the countries.

2 Find facts on the above items for each of the four countries. Don't forget, if the site has a search engine, use it.

3 Make a note of anything you particularly liked or disliked about the websites.

Task 3

1 Write down the websites that you found the best for finding information.

2 Make a note of the searches that produced good results and also those that caused you problems.

3 Where else could you find information, apart from the Internet?

4 What are the advantages and disadvantages of information from the Internet, compared to information from other sources?

▶ Skills help

Search engines, pages 97–98.

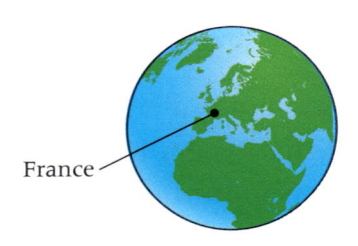

Canada

Singapore

France

Australia

Test centre

1 When should AND be used in a search?
2 What is a wild card search?
3 How could I find all the words that have the letters 'mee' in them from within a long document?

Unit 3.3
Structure of databases

In this unit you are going to learn about different types of database and how information is stored in them.

Information in databases

Behind every search engine is a large database. The information in the database has been stored in an organised way so that it can be easily found using search criteria.

Flat file database

A flat file database has only one table with all the information in it, as in the example below. A flat file database can be created using any database software, or spreadsheet package, such as MS Excel.

Title	Author	Publisher name	Address
A Pack of Lies	Geraldine McCaughrean	Heinemann	Halley Court
Adventures of Sherlock Holmes	A Conan Doyle	Penguin	79–80 Strand
Black Beauty	Anna Sewell	Penguin	79–80 Strand
Don't Make Me Laugh	David Kitchen	Heinemann	Halley Court
Dracula	Bram Stoker	Penguin	79–80 Strand
The Lord of the Ring – The Fellowship of the Ring	J R R Tolkein	HarperCollins	77–85 Fulham Palace Road
Fifty-fifty Tutti-frutti Chocolate-chip	Esther Menon	Heinemann	Halley Court
Frankenstein	Mary Shelly	Penguin	79–80 Strand
Harry Potter & the Chamber of Secrets	J K Rowling	Bloomsbury	38 Soho Square
Harry Potter & the Goblet of Fire	J K Rowling	Bloomsbury	38 Soho Square
Harry Potter & the Order of the Phoenix	J K Rowling	Bloomsbury	38 Soho Square
Harry Potter & the Philosopher's Stone	J K Rowling	Bloomsbury	38 Soho Square
Harry Potter & the prisoner of Azkaban	J K Rowling	Bloomsbury	38 Soho Square
The Hound of the Baskervilles	A Conan Doyle	Penguin	79–80 Strand
Macbeth on the Loose	Robert Walker	Heinemann	Halley Court
Our Day Out	Willy Russell	Heinemann	Halley Court
The Lord of the Ring – The Return of the King	J R R Tolkein	HarperCollins	77–85 Fulham Palace Road
The Lord of the Ring – The Two Towers	J R R Tolkein	HarperCollins	77–85 Fulham Palace Road

Unit 3.3

Task 1

Open Resource 3.3 Books and Publishers.

1. Use the **Sort** facility to find out how many books in the list are published by Heinemann.
2. The address for Penguin needs to be amended. Change the address in all the Penguin records to 80 Strand and save and close the file.
3. How many records did you have to change?

▶ Skills help

Sorting and filtering in Excel, pages 98–99.

Relational databases

A relational database stores data in separate tables. Each table holds data about just one aspect of the total information held. For example, a table could contain details about books such as the title, author and publisher. A second table could contain any details about the publishers, such as their address.

If data about a publisher changes, you only have to amend it once in the publishers' table, and not in every record for books from that publisher. This saves data input time and should reduce data input errors. If you were using a flat file database you would have to amend the record of every book from that publisher.

Any two tables in a relational database are linked by an item of data that is common to both tables.

Books	Publishers
Title Author Publisher's name	Publisher's name Address 1 Address 2 etc

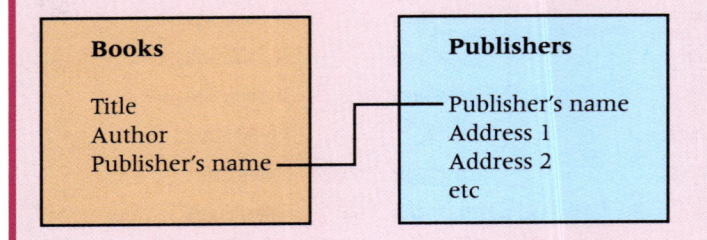

Task 2

Open Resource 3.3 Books 1 in a database program such as MS Access. You can see the two tables that have been created, **Books** and **Publishers**.

1. Open the **Books** table and see how the data has been entered. Close this table and open the **Publishers** table. This shows the rest of the data. Close the **Publishers** table.
2. Select **Queries** from the list on the left hand side of the window. Open the query, **Books & Publishers**. You will see how the database program pulls the information from the two tables together for you.
3. Close the query and open the **Publishers** table again. Amend Address 1 for Penguin – change it from 79–80 Strand to 80 Strand. Now close the table.
4. Re-open the **Books & Publishers** query. As you can see the address has been corrected in every Penguin record. How many records have you had to edit this time?
5. Which was easier to edit, the flat file database in Task 1 or this relational database?
6. Close the database.

Unit 3.3

> ⭐ MS Access automatically saves the record you are adding or editing as soon as you move the cursor to a different record, or close the table you are working on. **Resource 3.3 Books 1** is a copy of the **Resource 3.3 Books** file. If you want to make a fresh start at any time, copy **Resource 3.3 Books** and rename it *Books1.mdb*.

▶ **Skills help**

Sorting and filtering in Access, pages 99–101.

Module Task

You are going to **either** create a flat file database or work with a relational database to store the details of the characters you invented in Module 2, adding the name of the capital city of the country they each come from.

The flat file spreadsheet way

1. Open a new spreadsheet file and save it as Characters1.xls.

2. Enter the following column headings as the field names in your database.

   Character ID   Name   Gender   Age   City/town   Country   Capital city

3. Each character must have a unique ID. This means that if two of your character's had the same name and came from the same country, their records would still be unique because they would have different Character ID's. Your characters' IDs will be 1 – 4, enter these into column one.

4. Enter the character and country details to create the records. Save and close the file.

You will be able to add details of additional characters to this database, and search and sort the records to find out about individual characters.

▶ **Skills help**

Creating a relational database, pages 101–104.

The relational database way

🖱 Open **Resource 3.3 Characters 1**.

1. Open the **Characters** table and for each character you invented in the Module 2 enter their:
   - name
   - gender
   - age
   - city/town
   - country

   As you do this the program will automatically enter a Character ID.

2. Close the table (the data you have entered is automatically saved).

You now have a database that can be altered very easily, especially if you have to amend details about a country, or you want to move a character to a different country.

The **Resource 3.3 Characters 1** is a copy of the **Resource 3.3 Characters** file. If you want to make a fresh start at any time, copy **Resource 3.3 Characters** and rename it Characters1.mdb.

85

Unit 3.3

Producing queries

A query is created to bring data together from different tables in a relational database. You saw this earlier with the Books & Publishers query in Task 2.

Database programs have a routine for creating queries. For example in Access if you select **Queries** in the Database Window, you can then use a wizard to create the query. This allows you to select the fields you want to be in your query from the database tables.

Task 3

Open **Resource 3.3 Characters 2**.

1. With **Queries** selected you will find a query called **Where they live**. Open and view this query. Close the database.

2. Open your **Characters 1** database from the Module task. Open the **Countries** table and enter the school starting ages and school leaving ages that you found out in Unit 3.2.

3. Use the wizard to create a query that lists the names of your characters, their age and the age they would start and leave school. Give the query a suitable name.

Task 4

Your database needs to contain more data to make it realistic.

Use **Resource 3.3 Character data** to make a list of another twenty characters for the Character table in your database.

You will need this data in Unit 3.4.

Test centre

1. What is a flat file database?
2. What is a relational database?
3. What makes a relational database useful?

Unit 3.4
Searching for information using databases

In this unit you will learn how to change the look of a database to make it easier to use. You will use a database to search for information and produce a report.

Changing the look of datasheets

In a database anything shown in row and column format can be referred to as a datasheet, this is the same in Excel or Access. The format of a datasheet can be changed so that it appeals to a particular audience, or suits a particular purpose.

The font size, style and colour of the data in a datasheet can be changed. The colour of the background and gridlines can also be changed, and different cell effects can be used.

Characters : Table

Character ID	Name	Gender	Age	City/town	Country
1	Simone	F	13	Bordeaux	France
2	Francois	M	14	Paris	France
3	Jake	M	14	Vancouver	Canada
4	Luke	M	12	Toronto	Canada
5	Petra	F	13	Liverpool	UK
6	Harry	M	14	Exmouth	UK
7	Soo Lee	F	12	Singapore	Singapore
8	Mikki	F	13	Singapore	Singapore
9	Sidonie	F	13	Lille	France
10	Mark	M	14	Perth	Australia
11	Gemma	F	13	Ottawa	Canada
12	Jen	F	13	Sydney	Australia
13	Michael	M	13	Darwin	Australia
14	Denis	M	14	Toulouse	France
15	Vikram	M	14	Birmingham	UK
16	Mehta	F	13	Swansea	UK
17	Nester	F	12	Singapore	Singapore
18	Dilys	F	13	Glasgow	UK
19	Floyd	M	14	Singapore	Singapore
20	Rashmi	M	13	Brisbane	Australia
(AutoNumber)					

Countries : Table

Country	Capital city	Starting school age	School leaving age
Australia	Canberra		
Canada	Ottawa		
France	Paris		
Singapore	Singapore		
UK	London	4	16
		0	0

> ⭐ Changing the look of a datasheet can make it easier to use.

87

Unit 3.4

Task 1

The Excel way

1. Open the Characters1.xls file you created in Unit 3.3. Add details of all the characters you thought of at the end of Unit 3.3. Save the file.
2. Change the colour of the background of the datasheet.
3. Change the fonts and the layout style – perhaps you want to turn off the cell borders?
4. Change the alignment in the cells to make it easier to read.
5. Save and close the file.

Task 1

The Access way

1. Open your Characters 1 database that you created in the Module task of Unit 3.3. Open the **Characters** table and add the details of all the characters you thought of at the end of Unit 3.3.
2. With the table open, click on **Format** on the top menu bar and select **Datasheet**. Change the colour of the background and view it with and without the grid lines.
3. Close the datasheet formatting window, click on **Format** on the top menu bar and select **Font**. Experiment with changing the font, its colour, style and size.
4. Decide which formatting combination you like the best and format the second table in the same way.
5. Now ask a partner to add the details of their characters and any new countries to your database. Add yours to their database in return. Close the database.

▶ Skills help

Formatting datasheets in Excel, pages 104–105.

Formatting datasheets in Access, page 105.

Task 2

Open **Resource 3.4 Characters 3**.

1. Open the **Where they live (green red silver)** query. As you can see the presentation of a query can be changed in the same way as a datasheet can. Do you think this screen is very clear for the reader?
2. Close the query and click on **Forms** on the left hand side of the window. Open the **Characters** form. How do you think the form could be used?
3. Close the database.

Searching for information in a database

In the same way as a search engine is used to find information from the Internet, a database can be searched to find all the information on one topic. This is sometimes called 'running a query' or 'interrogating the data'.

There are several ways of searching for information in a database.
- Sorting to put the records in a particular order, e.g. alphabetically.
- Filtering so that only those records that match certain criteria are displayed, e.g. all names beginning with J.
- AND/OR queries, which allow you to combine more than one criterion in a search, e.g. all people that come from Canada and are male.

Skills help

Sorting and filtering in Excel, pages 98–99.

Sorting and filtering in Access, pages 99–101.

Module Task

1. Open either your **Characters1.xls** file in Excel or your **Characters 1** database in Access. If you are working in Access, open the **Characters** table.
2. Apply a filter that displays just the records of characters in the database that come from France.
3. Remove the filter.
4. Carry out a sort to list all of the records, with the highest Character ID number first.
5. Remove the sort and close the database without saving any changes.

Reports

The results of searches can be presented as **reports**. These reports allow you to bring the information together in a clear way for the end user. Reports can be produced in both Excel and Access.

Reports in Excel are normally created in a word processed document with a live link to an Excel file.

Unit 3.4

Reports in Access are created from the database. The fields that you want to appear in the document are selected in a Report Wizard. When the layout has been set up, the report can be sent straight to a word processing program where it can be edited like any other document.

Task 3

Reporting the Excel way

1. Open a new word processing document and also open your **Characters1.xls** file.
2. Apply a filter to find the records of all those characters that live in Singapore. Select these records and copy them.
3. Click in the word processing document where you would like the records displayed.
4. Use **Paste Special** to place the records from the linked Excel file into the word processing document.

▶ Skills help

Creating reports in Excel, page 106.
Creating reports in Access, pages 106–107.

Test centre

1. What can you change about the way your database looks?
2. What is a filter?
3. What is a report?

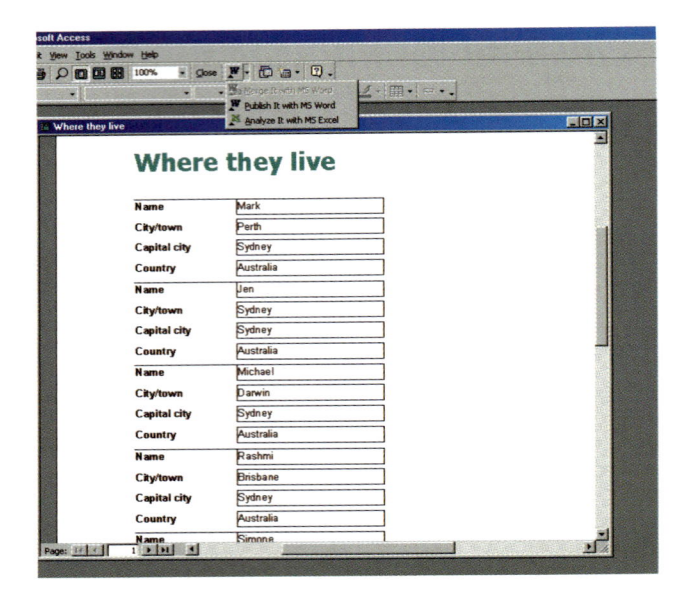

Task 3

Reporting the Access way

Open **Resource 3.4 Characters 3**.

1. Select **Reports** and you will find a report already created called **Where they live**. Open and view this report. Close the database.
2. Open your **Characters 1** database. Click on **Reports** on the left hand side of the window.
3. Use the **Reports Wizard** to produce a report that lists the names of your characters, their age and the age they would start and leave school in their country.

Ignore grouping levels and sorting options.

4. Select any layout, orientation and style and give the report any suitable name.
5. With the report open, go to the **OfficeLinks** icon on the top menu bar. Select **Publish It with MS Word**. The file will then open in Word.
6. Alter the layout of the report until you are happy with the way it looks.
7. Save and close the files.

90

Unit 3.5
Data about people

In this unit you are going to identify how the use of data about individual people is controlled.

Data protection

Data about living people is protected by law in a number of ways. The two main laws affecting the way that data can be used or stored are:
- The Freedom of Information Act 2000
- The Privacy and Electronic Communications (EC Directive) Regulations 2003

The Freedom of Information Act 2000 is designed to help provide people with the right to access information held about them and to find out what types of information are or can be held by the authorities.

The Privacy and Electronic Communications (EC Directive) Regulations 2003 provide protection against unwanted direct marketing activity by
- telephone
- fax
- electronic mail – this means text/video/picture messaging and email
- automated calling systems.

So what can you do to protect yourself?

As a company or person who wants to keep information about others

Anyone who wants to store **personal information** about others must be registered with the Data Protection Commissioner and follow the Principles of Data Protection. This means that:
- they have obtained consent from the person whose data is to be stored
- they have only collected the data for one of a list of legitimate purposes

Unit 3.5

- they have obtained the information fairly and lawfully
- the information is accurate and up-to-date
- they make sure that the data is protected by proper security
- they do not **misuse** the data and only use it for the registered purpose.

As a person who knows that data is being stored about them
People who know that data is being stored about them have the right to:
- see the information stored about themselves
- have the information corrected if it is wrong or **misrepresents** them
- in some cases claim compensation.

The laws cover data stored on paper, as well as purely electronic data. The Data Protection Commissioner has the right to inspect an organisation's computers to make sure that they are following the regulations.

Protecting against unwanted electronic direct marketing materials
To protect yourself against getting unwanted electronic communications, you need to register an objection by registering the telephone number with a government registration agency.

Task 1

Open **Resource 3.5 Data protection**.

1 *Write down a list of the information that you think the following organisations will have about you and your family.*
   - School
   - Doctors
   - Hospitals
   - Telephone companies
   - Supermarkets
   - TV Licencing Agency
   - Banks and building societies
   - Passport Agency

2 *How many of these organisations or companies need to register with the Data Protection Agency?*

The little box

When people buy goods, fill in forms, or answer questionnaires, there is often a little tick box somewhere on the form. Sometimes people are asked to tick the box if they agree to their information being made available to other companies, and sometimes they are asked to tick the box if they don't agree.

The company that has sold you the goods, or asked you to complete the form or questionnaire, can then sell this information about you to other companies. This is how the direct mailing companies gain access to mailing lists of target audiences.

The direct mailing companies also keep details of the people who respond to the mailing. So they now have another data file of new potential customers as well.

HACKERS

Computers can be accessed by people trying to find out other people's personal details, such as their credit card details. These people are called **hackers**. Computers can be protected from hackers using software called a firewall.

SPAM

The number of companies using email as the main method for communicating with their customers has increased a lot in recent years. Many companies offer customers the chance to receive their newsletters electronically, as wel las in paper form. Customers usually have the chance to say whether or not they want to be contacted by email.

Module Task

1. Imagine the characters in your web game are real people. Create a word processed report on how the data laws would affect you as the person responsible for putting their details into the computer?

2. One of the characters from your game contacts you about the information you hold about them. Create another word processed report on all of the things that you would need to do to make sure that you were complying with the data laws as described in this module.

However some companies have taken a different route and send out mass email messages through the use of SPAM. This sends messages to people's mailboxes that they have not asked for and may well not want to receive.

The new Privacy and Electronic Communications (EC Directive) Regulations 2003 will be able to stop most unwanted email messages. However this law can only be enforced if you know who sent the SPAM message.

Most SPAM messages can be avoided if people follow these simple tips.

- Do not post messages to newsgroups using your email address.
- Do not give your email address to an online retailer.
- Do not sign up for Internet services that ask for email addresses.
- Do not sending an email reply to the spammer asking them to remove you from their mailing list. Spammers often guess email addresses and they use your email reply to check that your email address is correct and will just send you more SPAM.
- Do not give out your e-mail address on your own website.
- Try setting up a second email address and only give this address to online retailers, etc.
- Make sure that your computer system is safe from hackers by using a firewall.

Task 2

1 Write a list of dos and don'ts as advice for Year 6 pupils who are about to start secondary school, about how they can protect themselves from unwanted email messages.

2 Open a word processing program and produce your list as a leaflet for the children.

Remember - if your audience is younger children you will have to use the correct type of words or images for them to understand what you are trying to tell them.

Test centre

1 What data is protected from misuse?
2 What do I have the right to do if I am worried about data that is being stored about me?
3 In ICT what is SPAM?

Module 3 Assignment

Image database

To complete Module 3 you are going to find images about the four countries that could be used in promotional material about your web game.

Brief
You should try to find the images from all sources available to you, for example:
- CD-ROMs
- the Internet
- databases available at libraries and other information centres.

Make a note about each of the sources of the images in terms of:
- how easy it was to find the image – if it was there at all
- the method of searching that you used.

The images that you need to find for each of the four web game countries are:

a) Images of native animals

b) National sports

c) National celebrations

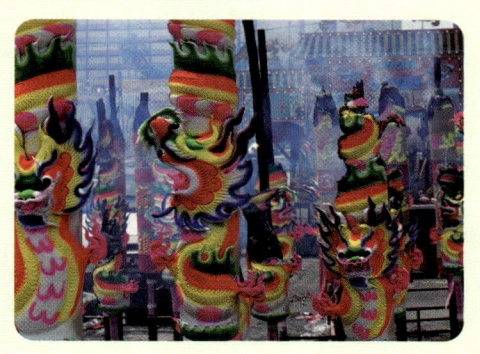

d) Typical foods

Some websites that might help can be found at

http://www.heinemann.co.uk/hotlinks.

It is a good idea to store detailed information about images, in case you need to refer back to it in the future. So you need to set up a catalogue for the images you have found.

Create a database listing as much information as possible about the images, for example the identification number of the image, which country it relates to, what it shows, where the image is stored, where you found the image, the photographer, the date of the photo, and any copyright issues related to the image.

Produce a report listing just the images from all four countries which relate to national celebrations.

Module 3 — Skills help

Text searches in Word

1. Select **Find** from the **Edit** menu.
2. The **Find and replace** dialogue box will appear. If the full dialogue box shown below does not appear click the **More** button.

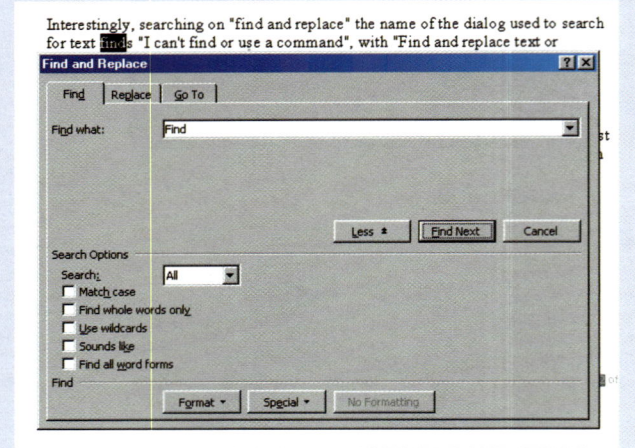

To search for the word 'Low' every time it appears in the Word document:

3. Type **Low** into the **Find what** box.

This search will find every time 'Low' appears in the document, but it will also find 'lower', 'flow', 'slow' and 'flower' etc.

4. To avoid this check the **Match case** and **Find whole words only** boxes in the **Search Options**, so that only the word 'Low' is found.
5. Click the **Find Next** button and the search will begin.

You can also select in what direction the document is searched from the **Search Options**.

The **Search** box opens with **All** showing. This starts the search from where the cursor is in the text, down through the text to the end, starts again at the beginning and continues until the whole document has been searched.

By changing **All** to **Up** or **Down**, the search either searches the document up from where the cursor is, or down from where the cursor is.

System searches

1. Click **Start**, **Find** and select **Files or Folders**.
2. The **Find: All Files** dialogue box will then open.

Searching on name

1. Enter the name or part of the name of the file or folder in the **Named** box.
2. Click the **Browse** button to select a particular folder to start searching in.
3. The setting **Include subfolders** means that the search will look in all the subfolders of the starting folder as well. Check this box if you want the subfolders to be searched as well.
4. If **Case Sensitive** is deselected in the **Options** menu it will not matter if the search item has the same capital letters as the file you are looking for. 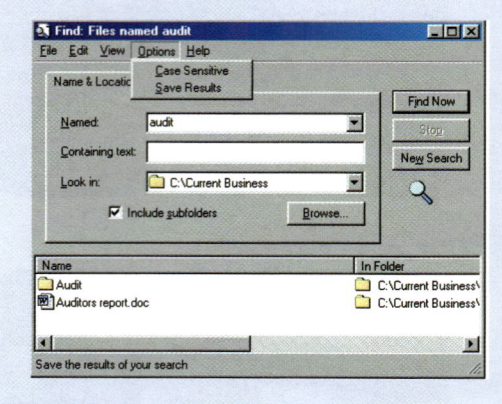
5. Click **Find Now**.
6. The names of any files or folders found that match the search criteria are listed in the dialogue window.

Searching on contents

A file can be searched for on some of is contents.

To find files containing the word 'financial', type **financial** into the **Containing text** box.

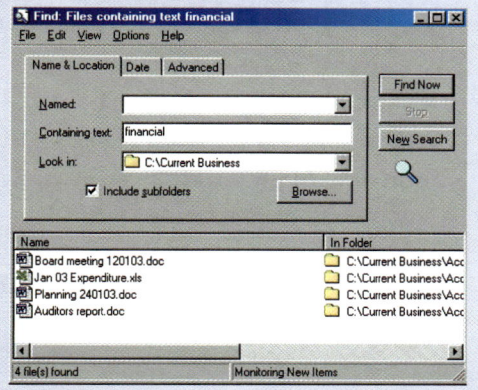

Searching the contents of files takes longer than searching on name.

Search engines

The most basic way a search engine can work is to find any of the words that you ask it to look for in a website.

For example, you want to find web pages about football stars having success and enter three words into the search box.

| football | star | success |

The results of the search would list:
- all pages containing the word 'football'
- all pages containing the word 'star'
- all pages containing the word 'success'
- any combination of these words.

This search has used the search criterion **OR**.

football **OR** star **OR** success

The web pages could have anything to do with football, including football makers, anything to do with stars, like astronomy, and pages on anything that had been a success!

Most search engines assume that you want a web page that contains all of these words. Google will add the instructions to find pages containing all the words for you. Search engines like Alta Vista expect you to add in the exact instructions that you want. This is done by putting a plus sign in front of each word.

| +football | +star | +success |

This search is saying that the page **must** contain the words

football **AND** star **AND** success.

Try out these ideas

1. Open a search engine like the one shown here.
2. Enter the three words into the search box.

This brings up 521,000 results with the first ones being spot on.

But by result number 281, the search is bringing up web pages that are nothing to do with what was needed.

3. If **NOT** is added into the search criteria, then a lot of the web pages will not be listed in the results.

Enter the following search.

| football **AND** star **AND** success **NOT** astronomy |

Skills 3

97

This gets rid of 21,000 of the results.

4 To get the exact information you want you need to use a group of words in " ". Only results where the words appear together in the same order will be returned.

Enter "football star has success".

No results! The "" search is best kept for groups of words that would normally come together, such as film or song titles.

Guide
- Think carefully about information you are trying to find.
- Search using words that are as specific as possible – and the more words the better.

Setting up a database in a spreadsheet

A database is made up of a number of records, each record contains a number of fields.

1 Enter the **field names** across the top of the worksheet as column headings. It is a good idea to make them bold or italic so they stand out.
2 Enter **record numbers** down the left hand side of the worksheet. Each record should have a unique number that is never repeated.

3 You can now enter your data. Click on a cell and start typing. You can enter either numeric or alphanumeric data.

Sorting and filtering in Excel

Sorting

1 Highlight the data you want to sort.
   NB It is very important that you highlight all the data in your database, including the record numbers, before you sort.
2 Click on **Data**, **Sort**.

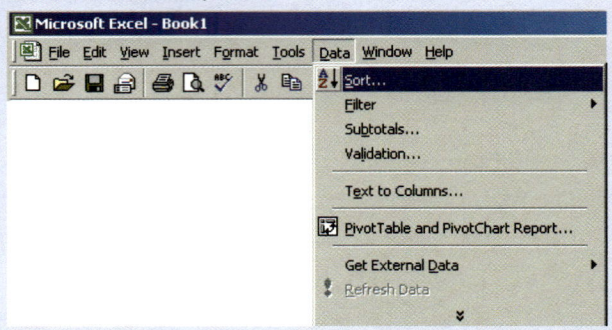

3 Click on the down arrow in the **Sort by** window and choose the first column that you want to sort by.

4 Click either the **Ascending** or **Descending** button.
5 Click on the down arrow in the **Then by** window and choose the second column that you want to sort by.
6 Click either the **Ascending** or **Descending** button.
7 If the data you have highlighted includes the field headings then click on the **Header row** button.
8 Click **OK**.

Filtering

1 Highlight the data you would like to filter.
2 Click on **Data**, **Filter**, **Auto filter**. A drop-down menu appears in each column heading.

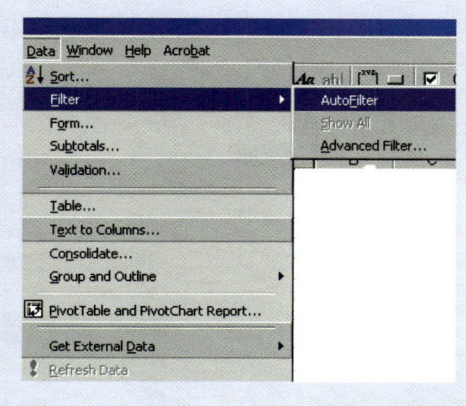

3 Click on the drop-down for the column you want to filter. A list of filtering options appears.

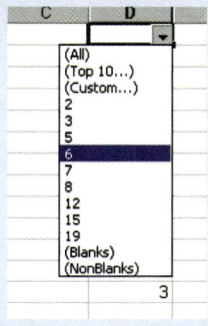

If you want to filter by one thing only:
4 Select it from the list.

If you want to filter by more than one of the things on the list:
5 Click on (Custom…) The **Custom AutoFilter** dialogue box appears.
6 Click on the top left list arrow to choose the type of filter.
7 Click on the top right list arrow to choose the data list.

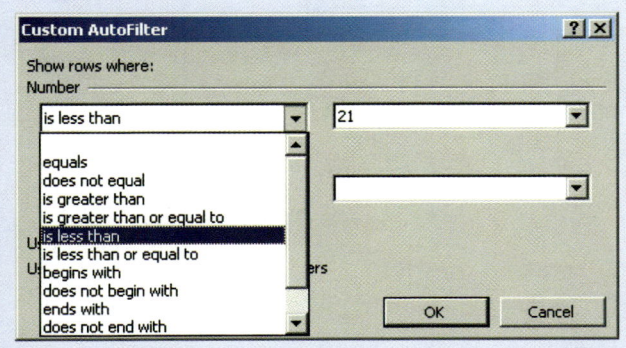

8 Enter your second set of selection criteria in the bottom two windows.
9 Click on the **And** button if you want to find only records which match *both* sets of selection criteria.
10 Click on the **Or** button if you want to find all records which match *either* one *or* the other selection criteria.
11 Click on **OK**.
12 Click away to deselect the data and view the filtered data.

Filtering more than one column at a time:

If you filter one column and then do another filter on another column, that is an AND search across both columns. You can carry on filtering as many columns as you want. As you add each new filter the computer will only find the records that match the filter criteria for *all* the filters you have set up.

Sorting and filtering in Access

Filtering

This example filters the Characters table so that only the records for characters from the UK are included.

1 Right click in the Country field of a record of someone from the UK and select **Filter by Selection**.

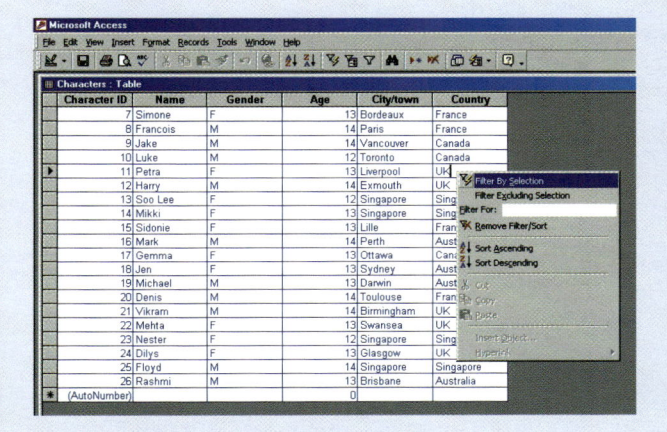

This filters out all characters who do not come from the UK.

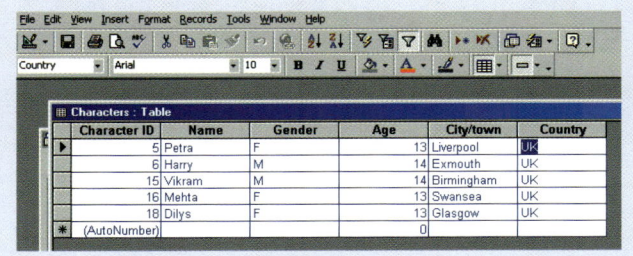

2. Selecting **Filter Excluding Selection** will filter out all similar records. So all records of characters from the UK are filtered out and all other records are displayed.

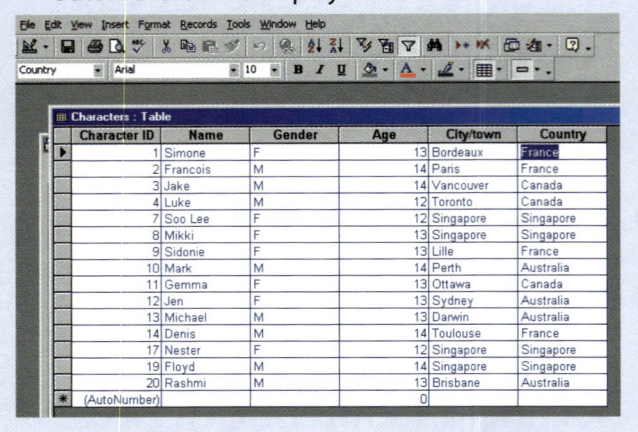

3. You can then further filter the data. To select only 14 year olds from the remaining countries displayed, right click in the Age field of someone aged 14. Then select **Filter by Selection** from the menu bar. This will filter the already filtered fields.

The filter will display just the 14-year-old characters who are NOT from the UK.

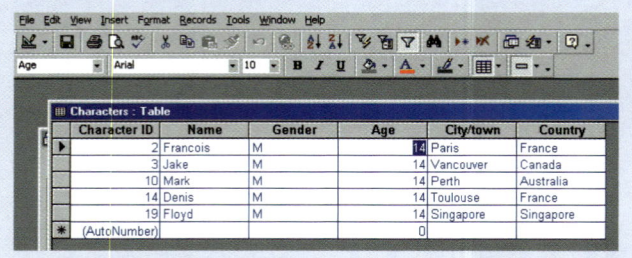

Saving a filtered table
If the table is saved with filters applied, the filters are saved as well. If you close and reopen the table all records are displayed again, but you can apply the filters again.

Click **Records** and select **Apply filter** in the menu bar or click the **Apply Filter** button and both filters are applied.

The **Apply Filter** button is ghosted if there are no filters in place.

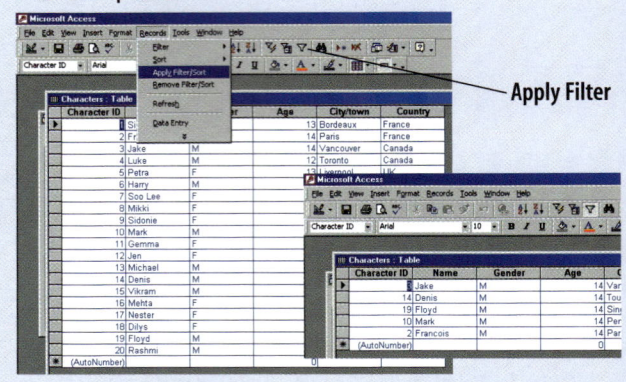

Removing filters
With filters applied, the **Apply Filters** button becomes the **Remove Filters** button. Click this **Remove Filters** button and the full data set is displayed again.

Changing filters
Display the full data set and apply a new filter. This removes any existing filters and just the new filter is applied.

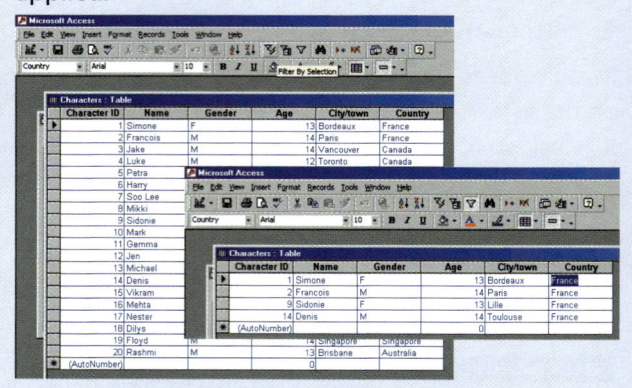

If you close the table *without* saving, the original filters will remain.

If you save the table with the new filter applied, the original filters will be replaced by the new filter.

Filters and queries
Queries can be filtered in just the same way as tables.

Sorting

Click in the field you want to sort on and click the **Sort Ascending** or **Sort Descending** buttons on the toolbar, or select **Records**, **Sort**, **Sort Ascending** or **Sort Descending**.

Multiple sorts

Select adjacent columns and click **Sort**. The table is sorted on the leftmost column first, then the next column and so on.

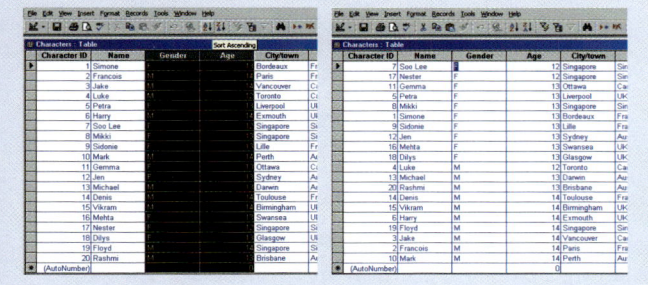

To sort on Country and then City/town these columns would have to be swapped over in the table. This can be done in **Design View** by clicking twice on one of the fields and dragging it to its new position.

Saving a sorted table

If a sorted table is saved, the sort is saved as well.

Removing a sort

To remove a sort select **Remove Filter/Sort** from the **Records** menu, or right click in the table and select **Remove Filter/Sort**.

Creating a relational database

1 Open a new database by clicking the **New** file icon. Then select the **Database** icon from the **General** tab.

2 Click **OK** and the **File New Database** dialogue box opens, which allows you to name and save the new database.

3 Give your database a name and click **Create**.

The Database window will then open.

Skills 3

4 Double click on **Create table in Design view**. This opens the Table window, displaying a new table.

5 Type in the field names in the **Field Name** column.

6 Select the **Data Type** for each field from the drop down list provided.

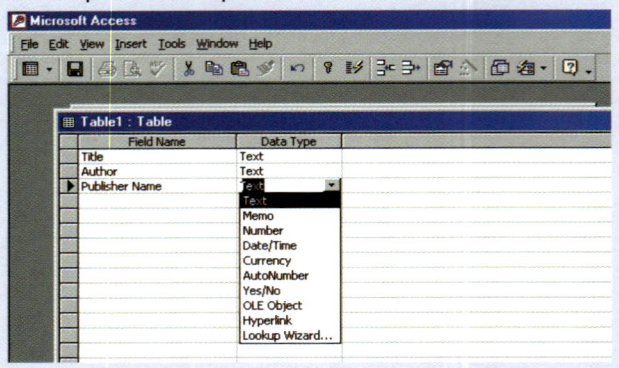

One of the fields must be set as the **Primary key** for the table.

7 Click the button at the end of the row to select the field.

8 Click the **Primary Key** icon.

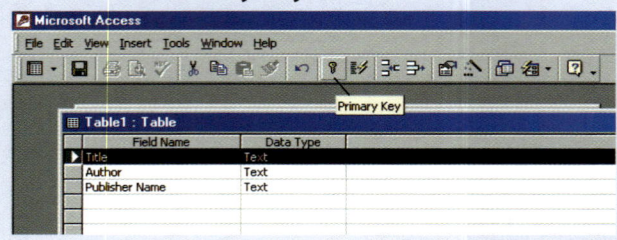

The primary key is used to identify each record and so you need to be certain that no two records will have the same entry in this field.

9 Click **Save** and name the table.

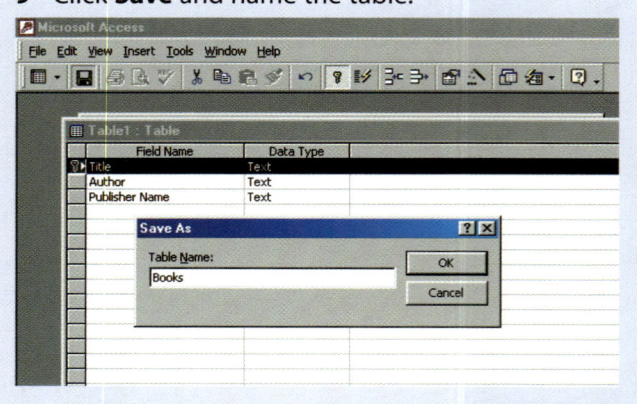

10 Click the **View** icon, this will close the table in **Design View** and open it in **Datasheet View** ready for data entry.

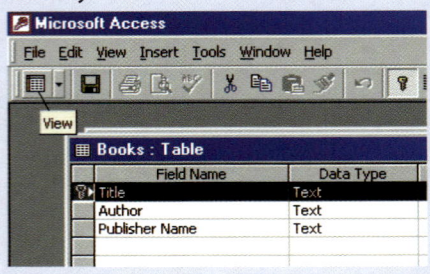

11 Enter data into the table.

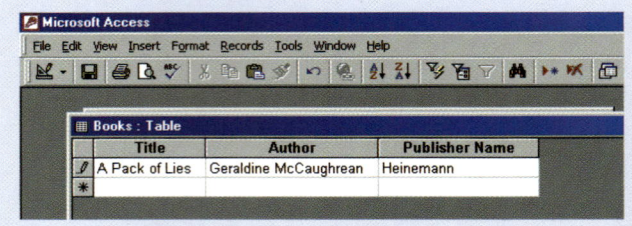

12 To resize the fields, click and drag the edge of the field column in the field name bar.

As you enter data into a record, a new record opens up.

The data is automatically saved as you move into the next record or close the table. If you have altered the field column widths, you will be prompted to save the new table layout as you close the table.

13 Click the **Close** button.

Other tables can be created in the same way.

Linking tables

The real trick with relational databases is that you can link or 'relate' the tables to one another and then bring data together from two or more tables.

1 Click the **Relationships** icon to open the **Relationships** window.

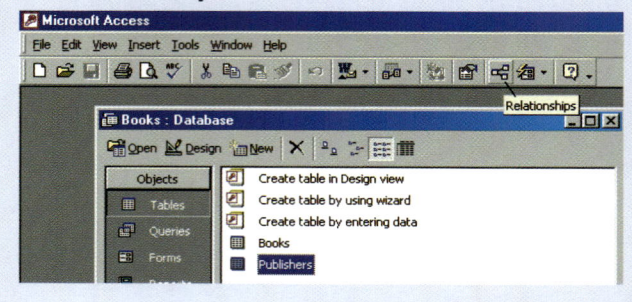

102

2 The **Show Table** dialogue box should open automatically. If it does not, click **Relationships**, **Show Table** in the menu bar.
3 Press the **Ctrl** key and click on both table names, so they are both highlighted.

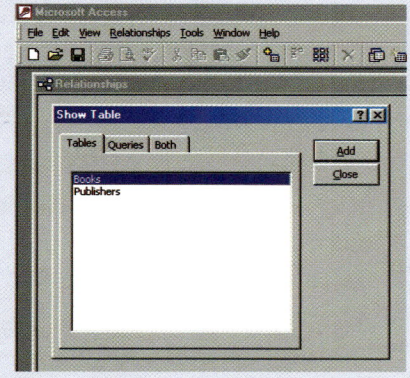

4 Click the **Add** button.

The tables will be displayed.

5 Close the **Show Table** dialogue box.
6 Click on a field in one of the tables and drag over a field in the other table, and release. The **Edit Relationships** dialogue box will open.

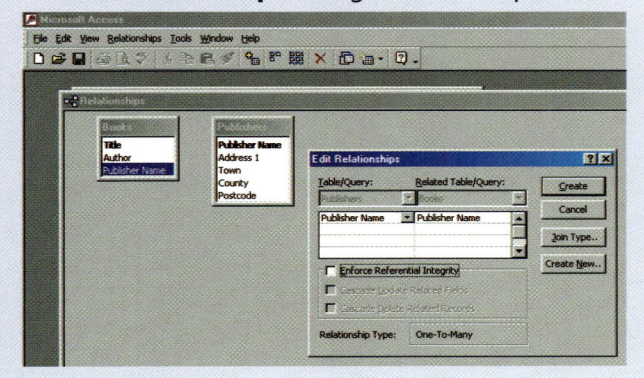

7 Click **Create**.

The link, or relationship, is made and displayed.

8 Save the relationship and close the **Relationships** window.

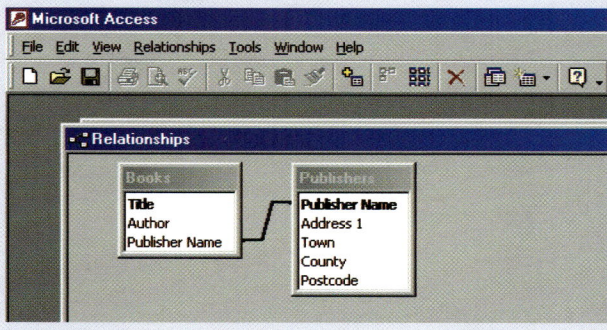

Creating a query

1 With **Queries** selected in **Objects** in the database window, double click **Create query by using wizard** to open the **Query Wizard** dialogue box.
2 Click the >> button to move all the Books table fields into the **Selected Fields** box.

3 Select a table from the drop down list in the **Tables/Queries** box.
4 Select all the fields using the >> button.

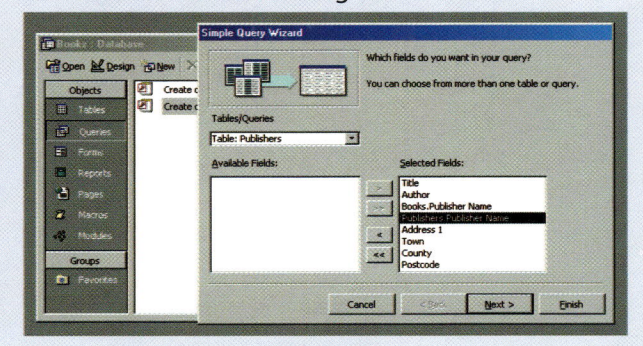

5 Remove any fields that you don't want in the query using the < button to remove it from the **Selected Fields** box.

103

Skills 3

6. Click the **Next** button and enter a name for the query.

7. Click **Finish** to view the query.

Changing the way your datasheet looks

In Excel
Changing the font appearance
1. Click in the cells you want to change.
2. Click on **Format**, **Cells**. The **Format Cells** dialogue box opens.

3. Click on the **Font** tab.

4. Scroll down and choose the options you want in the following windows:
   Font
   Font style
   Size
   Underline
   Colour
5. Click to choose any **Effects** such as strikethrough.
6. Click on **OK**.

Quick formatting of font style and size
1. Click in the cells you want to change.
2. To change font style, click the down arrow in the **Font** window on the **Formatting** toolbar and choose the font you want.

3. To change the font size, click the down arrow in the **Font size** window on the **Formatting** toolbar and choose the size you want.

Adding backgrounds and borders
1. Click in the cells you want to change.
2. Click on **Format**, **Cells**. The **Format Cells** dialogue box opens.

To add borders:
3. Click on the **Border** tab.

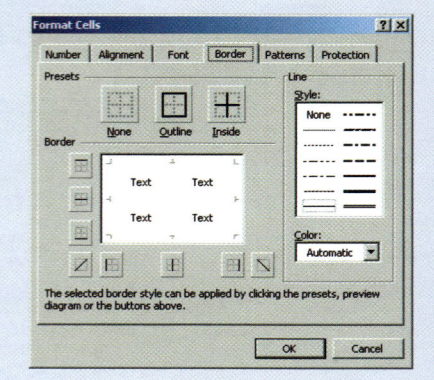

104

Skills 3

4 Either choose from one of the preset options, or click on the diagram to choose where you want your borders to go.
5 Select the **Border style** from the list on the right.
6 Click on the down arrow in the colour window and choose a colour.
7 Click on **OK**.

To add background colours and patterns:
8 Click on the **Patterns** tab.

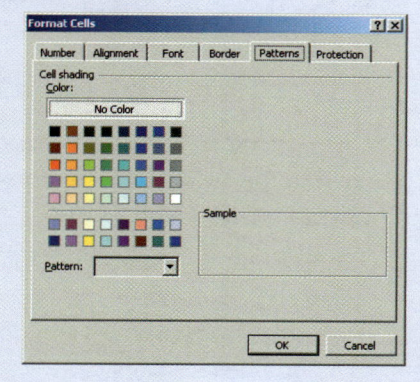

9 Click on the colour you want.
10 Click on the down arrow on the **Pattern** window and choose a pattern if you want to.
11 Click on **OK**.

In Access
The **Formatting** toolbar offers the following buttons.

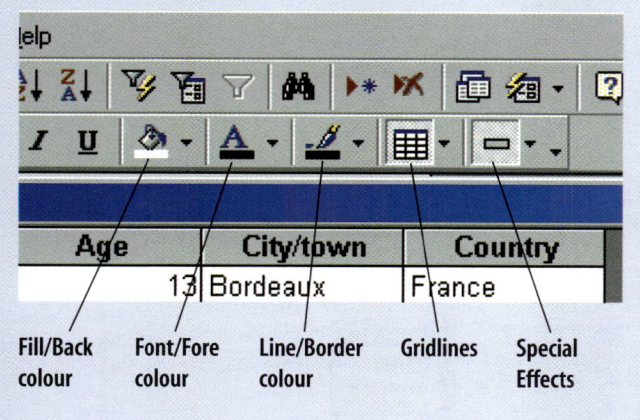

Fill/Back colour | Font/Fore colour | Line/Border colour | Gridlines | Special Effects

Colour
Each of the colour buttons offers a palette from which to choose. Just click on the colour you want.

Font and gridline colours can also be changed.

Gridlines
Using the **Gridlines** button you can switch gridlines on and off.

Special effects
The **Special Effects** button offers a **Raised** or **Sunken** effect for the datasheet cells as opposed to the default flat style. Here the cells are raised.

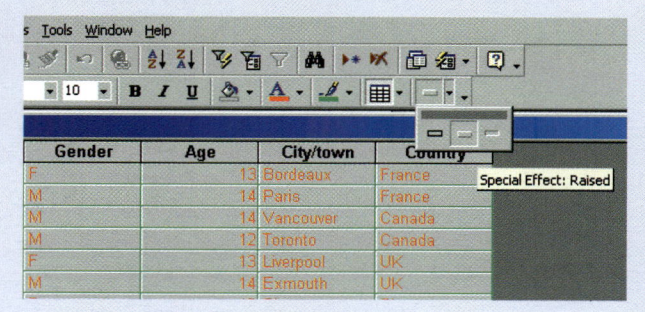

105

Skills 3

Creating reports

In Excel

1. Highlight the data in the spreadsheet that you want to appear in your report.
2. Click on **Edit**, **Copy**.
3. Switch to the word processor
4. Click in the place you want the data to be displayed.
5. Click **Edit**, **Paste Special**. The **Paste Special** dialogue box opens.
6. Click on **Paste Link**.

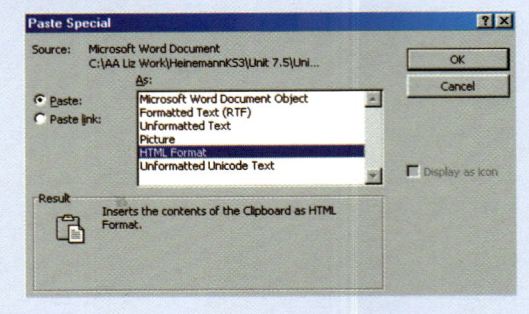

This will maintain a link between the data file and the document.

In Access

For this example the sample database **Characters 2** has been used.

1. Select **Reports** from the **Objects** list in the database window and double click **Create report by using wizard**. 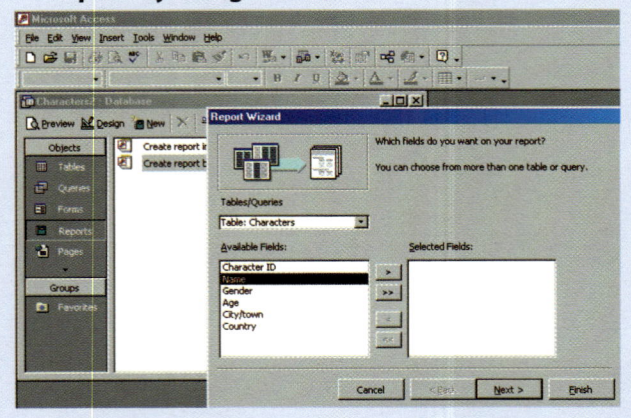
2. Select the **Name** field in the **Tables/Queries** box.
3. Move it to the **Selected Fields** box by clicking the > button.
4. Move the **City/town** field in the same way.
5. Select the **Countries** table in the **Tables/Queries** box.

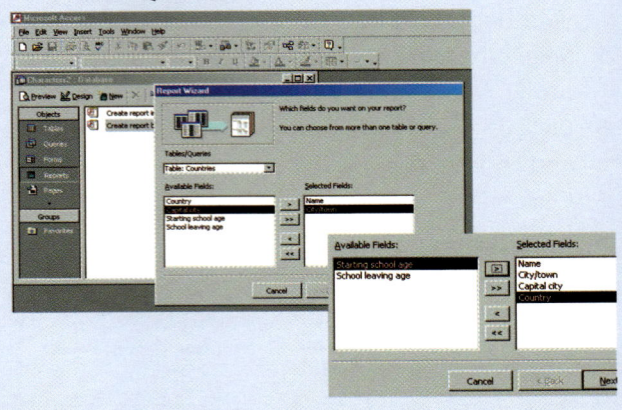

For the **Capital city** field to be next in the report, move it to the **Selected Fields** box before the **Country** field is moved across.

6. When all the fields required for the report are selected click **Next**.
7. Keep clicking **Next** until you get to the **Layout** dialogue box.
8. Select **Columnar** and select **Portrait**. 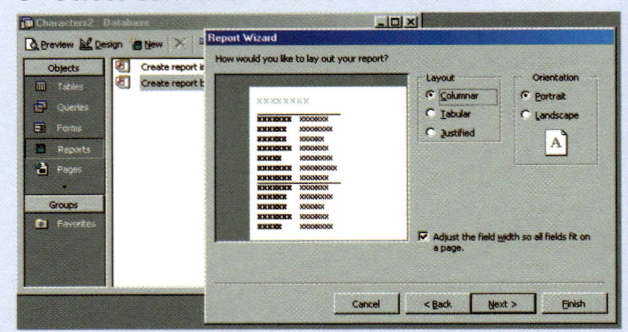
9. Click **Next**.
10. Select the **Casual** style
11. Click **Next** and enter a title for the report.

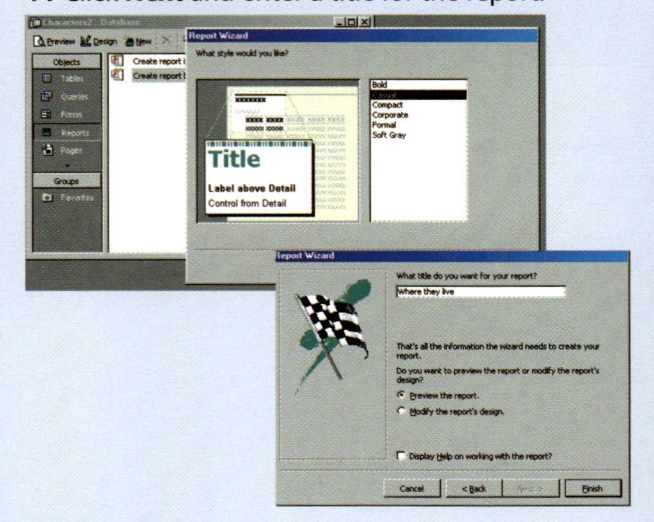

12 Select **Preview the report** and click **Finish**.
13 Preview the report and send for editing to Word by selecting **Publish with MS Word** from the **OfficeLinks** button menu.

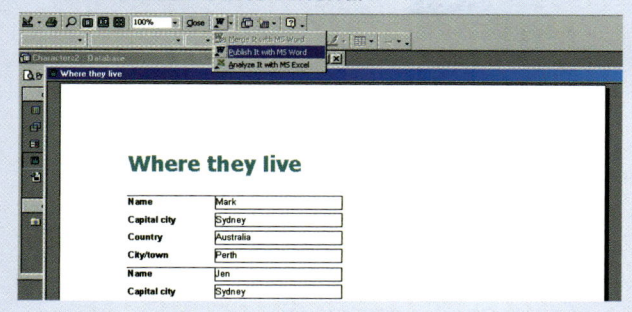

14 Word opens automatically with an *.rtf* version of the report. The report can now be edited and formatted as required.

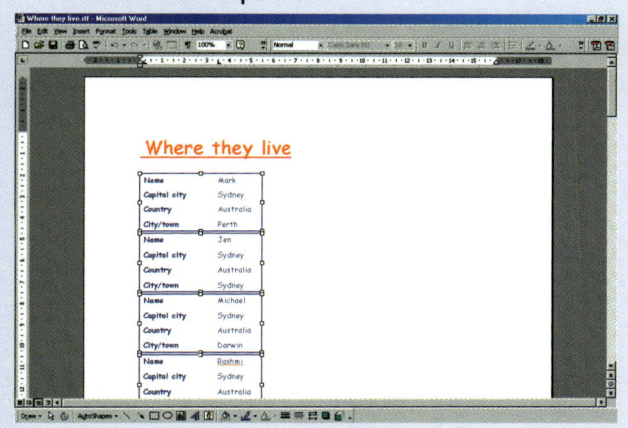

Using a query in creating a report

You can also create a report from a query.

1 Select **Queries** from the **Objects** list in the database window and double click **Create report by using wizard**.
2 Select the query in the **Tables/Queries** box.
3 Use >> button to select all the fields you want to appear in the report.

4 Follow the same process as before to produce the report.

Module 4
Models and presenting numeric data

Learning Targets

In this module you are going to find out how software can be used to develop models that can be used to simulate different journeys. You are going to do this by looking at the distances between the main cities in four countries. These are:
- Australia – Sydney
- France – Paris
- Canada – Vancouver
- Singapore – Singapore

In Module 4 you are going to learn:

How to use spreadsheet models to answer 'What if' questions by changing variables	See pages 112–114
How to use the Goal Seek function to help answer 'What if' questions	See page 113
About inputs, processes and outputs from a spreadsheet model	See pages 117–119
About relative and absolute cell references	See page 118
About using charts to display the outputs from a spreadsheet model	See pages 119–120
How to alter and refine models to make them user friendly	See pages 121–124
How to use drop-down menus to speed up data entry	See page 122
How to edit charts and graphs	See page 123
How to generate random numbers to test a spreadsheet model	See page 124
About the use of online models and simulations, such as interactive games	See page 127
About how data files can be protected	See pages 128–129

What are your targets for this module?

To achieve a level 4 in this module you will need to   **level 4**
- Use a spreadsheet model to make predictions and answer 'What if' questions by changing the values of variables (the trial and improvement method)
- Identify the rules within a spreadsheet model and explain what they do
- Enter numbers and text into a spreadsheet model and use formatting to improve the way it looks
- Enter formulae to express the rules in a model and check that the model works
  Create charts to help the user understand a model
- Use a model to draw conclusions

Learning Targets 4

To achieve a level 5 in this module you will need to — *level 5*
- Add more variables to a model to make it more realistic in order to make predictions and answer 'What if' questions
- Make use of absolute cell references within a model
- Use a model to draw conclusions. Explain your conclusions clearly for a target audience, including the use of charts and graphs
- Evaluate your model and suggest possible improvements

To achieve a level 6 in this module you will need to — *level 6*
- Improve your spreadsheet model by changing variables and rules to make it more realistic
- Use the Goal Seek function and explain how it can help with answering 'What if' questions
- Use the random number function to generate data to test a model
- Use software tools such as drop-down lists to speed up data entry into a model and make it more accurate
- Check how well your spreadsheet model works by comparing it with information from other sources

What do you know already?

Model
A model is a set of instructions that represents a real-world event or object. Models can be created on a computer using many different programs, e.g. spreadsheets.

Simulation
A simulation is what happens when you run a computer model. Simulations can be used to answer 'What if' questions.

Formulae
Formulae are used to carry out calculations or different actions with data in a worksheet: =SUM(D9:D15) is a formula to add up data in the cells between D9 and D15.
=RANDBETWEEN(5,10) is a function that will generate a **random number** between 5 and 10.

Random numbers. Models can make use of random numbers to test that the model is working correctly. A random number is one that the computer generates, not the user. The numbers can be set to be generated within a particular range, such as between five and ten.

Learning Targets 4

Spreadsheets

Spreadsheet programs such as MS Excel are made up of **worksheets**. These worksheets can be grouped into **workbooks**.

Worksheets. These are files where data is entered into rows and columns. *Charts* can then be drawn from the data.

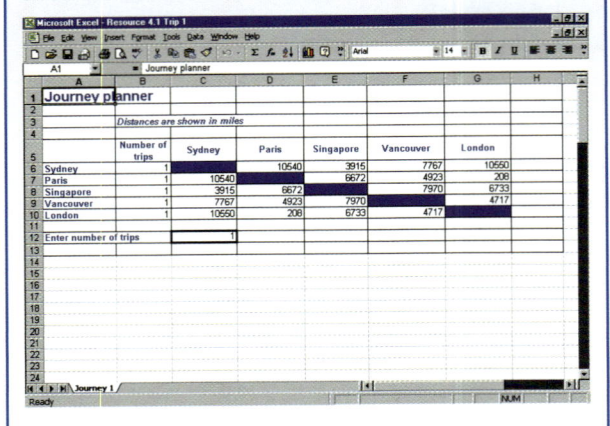

Workbook. A series of worksheets make up a workbook.

Charts. These can be produced to display data from a worksheet. A chart can be set up to be displayed in the same worksheet or as a separate sheet. Charts within the same spreadsheet display changes in the input data automatically.

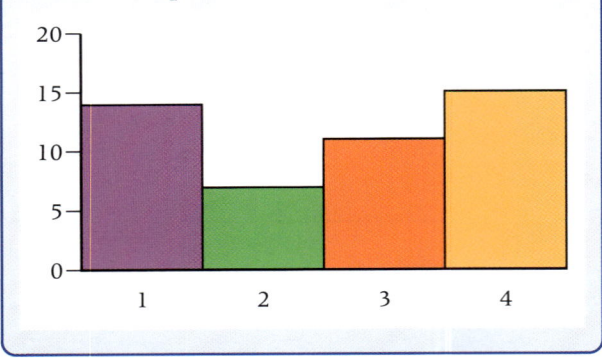

Task

You are going to set up a model to display a chart showing temperatures for a week in four countries:
- Australia
- France
- Canada
- Singapore

Open **Resource 4 Heat** in a spreadsheet program.

1. In cell **B8** enter the formula =**MIN(B3:B6)**. Copy the formula across all cells in this row.

2. In cell **B10** enter the formula =**MAX(B3:B6)**. Copy this formula across all cells in this row.

3. Create a chart to show the maximum temperatures for Wednesday.

4. Create a chart to show the minimum temperatures for Saturday.

5. Change the temperatures in some of the cells, what happens to the charts?

Unit 4.1
Using models to find solutions

In this unit you are going to revise your use of a spreadsheet as a model and use different methods of finding solutions to questions.

So to refresh your memory ...

A model is a set of instructions that represents a real-world event or object. Models can be created on a computer using many different programs, including spreadsheets. A model consists of inputs, rules and outputs.

	What this means	What it looks like in a spreadsheet	Effects of changing it
Inputs	The things you know about before you start	The numbers or variables which you input	Can be changed within a model to see what happens
Rules	What the model can and cannot do	The calculations (written as formulae)	If you change the rules the model changes
Outputs	What happens when you apply rules	The answers to the calculations	Will change if either the inputs or the rules are changed

Models are used to predict what could happen in real life situations, or to test out various possible solutions to a problem. You can use a model to ask 'What if...?' questions by changing the variables or the formulae.

'So how else could 2+2 = end?'

Unit 4.1

The advantages of using software such as spreadsheets to create models are:
- speed
- accuracy
- automatic calculations
- data can be changed easily.

A model can contain a very large number of different calculations, with many variables. Clear layout and presentation are important to make the model easy to use.

Making software do the work

Formulae can be set up in a model to help you do the work. If you have to find an answer to a question such as 'How many…?', 'How long…?', 'How high….?' simple formulae can help.

	A	B	C	D	E	F	G	H
1	**Journey Planner**							
2		Distances are shown in miles						
3			from		from	from	from	from
4	to	Number of trips*	Sydney	Total distance travelled to or from Sydney	Paris	Singapore	Vancouver	London
5	Sydney	1			10540	3915	7767	10550
6	Paris	1	10540	10540		6672	4923	208
7	Singapore	1	3915	3915	6672		7970	6733
8	Vancouver	1	7767	7767	4923	7970		4717
9	London	1	10550	10550	208	6733	4717	
11	*Trips are one-way only so a return journey would count as 2 trips							

Cell D9 = =B9*C9

In this example formulae have been set up in cells D6 to D9 to calculate the total distance travelled. This is done by multiplying the distance between Sydney and the other cities by the number of trips made.

The formula to calculate the total distance travelled between Sydney and London for a number of trips is D9 = B9*C9.

Quite often in modelling you know the result you want to get and you need to use the model to see how to get there. For example, if you know you have £10 to spend you might want a model to work out how many things you could buy with it. There are a number of techniques you can use to do this.

Task 1

Open **Resource 4.1 Trip 1** in a spreadsheet program.

1. Find the cells in the spreadsheet where formulae have been used and those where values have been entered.

2. There is a pattern to these different cells. Sketch the pattern you find and label where formulae are used and where values have been entered.

3. Do any of the formulae need data from other cells? Is there a pattern to this?

4. Change some of the entered values in the spreadsheet. (Do NOT save the changes.) Describe what happens when you change these values.

5. It takes time to work out and enter formulae. Explain why it is worth having formulae in the spreadsheet.

Unit 4.1

Trial and improvement

Look again at the journey planner model shown. Imagine you needed to know how many trips would have to be completed between London and Sydney before 35,000 miles has been travelled. To work this out you can increase the value in cell B9 until the value in cell D9 is greater than 35,000.

▶ *Skills help*

Using trial and improvement, page 132.

Goal Seek

The whole point of setting up a computer model is to let the software do the work. There are a range of different tools available that can help make the model more effective, one of them is called **Goal Seek**.

Goal Seek allows the user to set up a 'How much and how many would it take?' type of question, and then gets the software to work out the answer.

For example 'How many trips between Paris and Vancouver would I need to make before I have travelled 35,000 miles?'

▶ *Skills help*

Using Goal Seek, pages 132–133.

Unit 4.1

Trial and improvement or Goal Seek?

The main differences between these two methods are:

Trial and improvement:
- You input data and see what happens.
- It can take a long time.

Goal Seek:
- The software uses data already in the model and provides output data that will lead you to the answer.
- It is much quicker.

Module Task

Free flights are available to travellers after they have flown for 35,000 miles. You are going to find out how many trips it will take for someone to get a free flight if they travel regularly between Sydney and London. (A trip is a one-way journey.)

Open **Resource 4.1 Trip 2**.

Column C shows the distances between Sydney and the other cities.

Column D shows the total distances travelled between Sydney and the other cities for the number of trips entered in the matching cell in column B.

For example, cell D9 shows the total distance travelled between Sydney and London for the number of trips entered in cell B9.

1. Alter the number in cell **B9** until the value in cell **D9** becomes greater than 35,000.
2. Save the file as Answer.xls.
3. Check your answer with your partner.

Open **Resource 4.1 Trip 2** again.

Column E shows the distances between Paris and the other cities.

Column F shows the total distances travelled between Paris and the other cities, for the number of trips entered in the appropriate cell in column B.

1. How many journeys between Vancouver and Paris would I have to make to qualify for a free flight?

   Use Goal Seek to find the answer to this question by following these steps:
   a. Click in cell **F8**.
   b. Go to **Tools** and select **Goal Seek**.
   c. When the dialogue box appears enter 35,000 in the target box.
   d. Click in the **By changing cell** box and then click in cell **B8**.
   e. Click **OK**.

2. Write down the value that appears in cell **B8**. The number of trips to qualify will be the next highest whole number.

3. Cancel **Goal Seek** when you have written down the answer.

4. Does it look about right? Check with a partner to see what value they have.

5. Now use **Goal Seek** to find out the answer to these questions.
   - If I've made three trips between Vancouver and Sydney, how many more do I have to make before I get the free flight?
   - I've made three RETURN trips between Singapore and Paris and want to know whether I can travel free next time?

THINK how many trips would that mean in total?

Task 2

Details of a sixth city need to be added into the model.

The details are:
Colombo in Sri Lanka
Distance to Sydney = 5437 miles
Distance to Paris = 5291 miles
Distance to Singapore = 1699 miles
Distance to Vancouver = 8315 miles
Distance to London = 5401 miles

🖱 Open **Resource 4.1 Trip 2** again.

1. Add the details into the model, making sure that you apply the formulae to the correct cells.

2. Save your file as Trip3.xls.

▶ Skills help

Adding new entries into a spreadsheet, page 132.

Task 3

If you travel east from London you will reach the following cities in the order shown.

| London | 208 | Paris | 6672 | Singapore | 3915 | Sydney | 7767 | Vancouver | 4717 | London |

The numbers in red are the distances travelled.

Since the world is round, keep going and you can end up back in London!

🖱 Look at **Resource 4.1 Trip 2**.

The spreadsheet gives the shortest distances between each pair of cities. But you can travel either way around the world to get from any one city to any other city. For example you could go from Paris to London via Singapore, Sydney and Vancouver!

Could the model be developed to work out the distances between each pair of cities going the long way around? How?

Test centre

1. What is a computer model?
2. What two things could happen when a cell value changes?
3. What does Goal Seek help you to do?

Unit 4.2
Developing a new model

In this unit you are going to create a new model using spreadsheet software.

Preparation for modelling

'I must look my best for the camera'.

Before you start to create a new model, there are some questions you need to consider:
- What is the model for?
- What will the model do?
- Who is going to be using the model?
- What data will form the inputs to the model?
- What rules will the model follow?
- What is the clearest way to display the outputs of the model?

Case study

A local youth group would like to send groups of children on activity holidays. They have researched some information about holiday providers.

The youth group leaders would like you to create a model to help them decide which of the holiday providers offers the best value for groups of children.

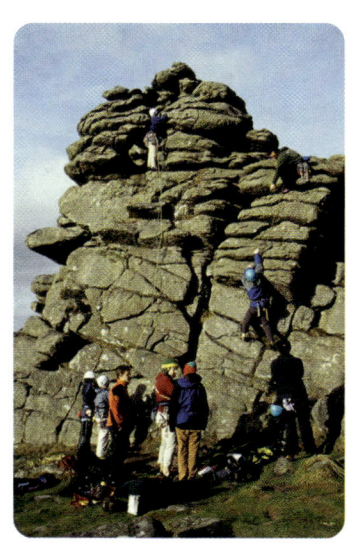

Task 1

Write down in your own words:
- *what you think the model is for*
- *what it will do*
- *who will be using the model.*

116

Inputs to a model

The inputs to your model can come from various places. Some inputs may be information that does not change once it has been put into the model. Other inputs need to be changed to see what happens. These are called variables.

Processes in a model

The processes in a spreadsheet model are the calculations that are carried out on the data. They are written down as formulae. To create your model you will need to write formulae that:
- add and subtract numbers
- multiply numbers together
- calculate percentages
- use cell references.

Task 2

Look at **Resource 4.2 Holidays 1**. It shows price information about six holiday providers.

1. Which fee is payable for every booking made?
2. What calculation would you need to do to find the cost for three children?
3. Explain in your own words what 'group discount' means.
4. What calculation would you need to do to find the total cost for 14 children?
5. Does the North Wales holiday provider encourage groups to attend? In what way?

Case study

Your model needs to work out the total cost of sending different numbers of children in groups. Different holiday providers offer different deals. For example some offer a discount if 10 or more children go in a group.

▶ Skills help

Writing formulae, pages 134–135.
Resource 4.2 Formulae.

Unit 4.2

Module Task

Open **Resource 4.2 Holidays 2** and **Resource 4.2 Holidays 2 questions**.

1. Write down in words the calculation that needs to go in cell **F3**. Then write it as a formula into the spreadsheet. What happens? Did you get the answer you expected?

2. Change the number of children from 1 to 6 (remember it must be the same number for all the holiday venues, so you need to copy and paste it down the column). Look at what happens to the result in cell **F3**.

3. Look at columns **H** to **K** which calculate costs for group bookings of 10 or more children.

4. Write down in words the calculations that need to go in cells **I3** and **K3**. Then write them as formulae into the spreadsheet.

5. When you are happy with the formulae in cells **F3**, **I3** and **K3**, copy and paste them down the rows to cover the other venues.

6. Use the group bookings model to calculate which venue offers the best value for a group of 12 children.

7. Save the file as Holidaysmodel.xls.

Absolute cell references

Cell references usually change to match their new positions when you copy and paste formulae. They are sometimes called **relative cell references** because they change relative to their new position. An **absolute cell reference** does not change when the formula is copied and pasted to a new position.

To make an absolute cell reference, you type $ in front of each bit of the reference, for example $C$3. This does not mean it is American currency – it just tells the computer not to change the reference when it is moved.

Absolute cell references are useful if you want lots of different formulae to include the same cell reference.

$$$$$

Task 3

1. Open your **Holidaysmodel.xls** file. Save it with a new filename – Holidaysmodelv1.xls.

2. In cell **E2** type a number between 1 and 9.

3. In cell **E3** type =$E$2.

4. Copy and paste cell **E3** down the rest of column **E**. Notice that the absolute cell reference does not change.

5. Go back to cell **E2** and change the number. Look what happens to all the other numbers in column **E**.

6. Do the same procedure in column **J**.

7. Save and close the file.

▶ *Skills help*

Cell references, page 135.

Outputs from the model

The outputs from a model are the 'answers' to the calculations. In the model you have been working on, the outputs are in cells F3-F8 and K3-K8.

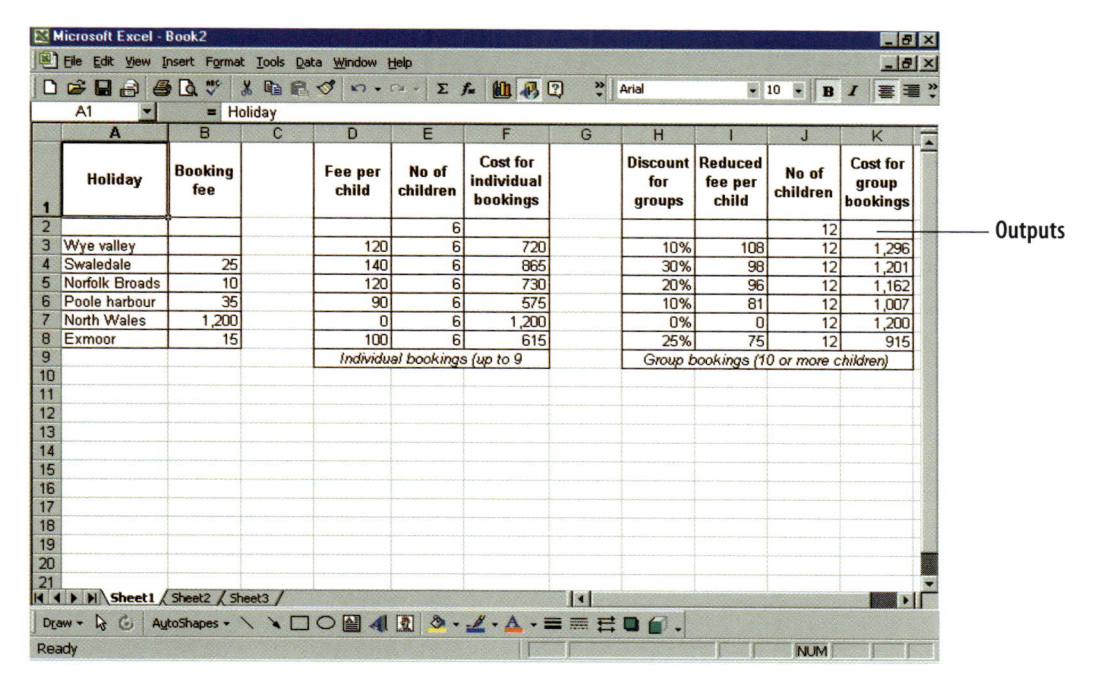

Holiday	Booking fee	Fee per child	No of children	Cost for individual bookings	Discount for groups	Reduced fee per child	No of children	Cost for group bookings
			6				12	
Wye valley		120	6	720	10%	108	12	1,296
Swaledale	25	140	6	865	30%	98	12	1,201
Norfolk Broads	10	120	6	730	20%	96	12	1,162
Poole harbour	35	90	6	575	10%	81	12	1,007
North Wales	1,200	0	6	1,200	0%	0	12	1,200
Exmoor	15	100	6	615	25%	75	12	915

Individual bookings (up to 9)   Group bookings (10 or more children)

Using charts to display the outputs

Charts are often a good way to display outputs so that they can be easily understood.

Look at these two screens.

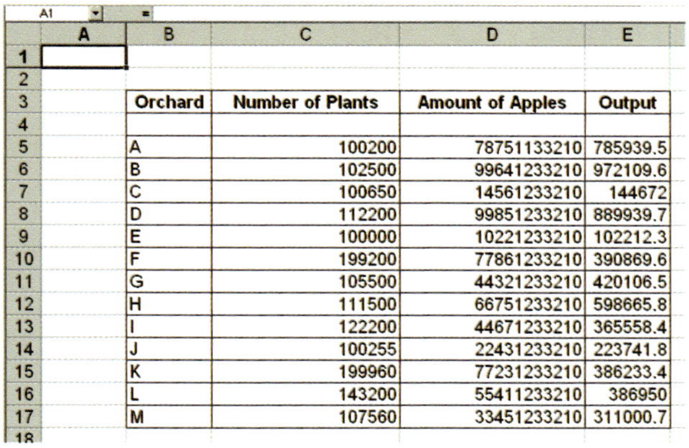

Orchard	Number of Plants	Amount of Apples	Output
A	100200	78751133210	785939.5
B	102500	99641233210	972109.6
C	100650	14561233210	144672
D	112200	99851233210	889939.7
E	100000	10221233210	102212.3
F	199200	77861233210	390869.6
G	105500	44321233210	420106.5
H	111500	66751233210	598665.8
I	122200	44671233210	365558.4
J	100255	22431233210	223741.8
K	199960	77231233210	386233.4
L	143200	55411233210	386950
M	107560	33451233210	311000.7

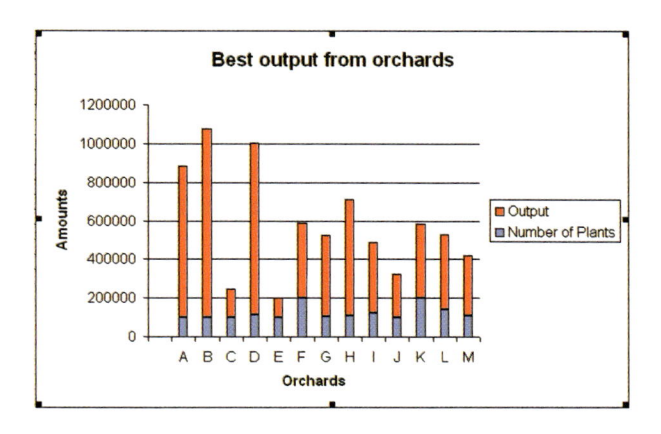

If you had to say which orchard was giving the farmer the best results, which is easier to understand – the spreadsheet or the chart?

Unit 4.2

Updating data in a chart

When a chart is created in a spreadsheet, as the data in the spreadsheet changes the data displayed in the chart also changes, so the chart changes.

This is a useful tool when demonstrating what effect changing a variable in a model has on the outcome.

Task 4

1. Open your **Holidaysmodel.xls** file.
2. You are going to create two charts to display the costs of sending children to the different venues. One chart will use costs from the individual bookings model, and the other will use costs from the group bookings model. Think about which columns of data you need in order to make each chart.
3. The series should be in rows. Make sure the labels are clear.
4. Place the charts in the same worksheet.
5. Experiment with changing the numbers of children in the model. What happens to the chart?
6. Use the models and the charts to decide which venue offers the best value for booking 7 children and 18 children.
7. Save and close the file.

Task 5

Imagine you are the youth group leader. You have just seen the model for the first time.

Working with a partner write down three good things about the model, and three things that you think could be improved.

Test centre

1. What is a variable?
2. What is a relative cell reference?
3. How do you write an absolute cell reference?

Unit 4.3
Using and extending the model

In this unit you will learn about ways to improve a model and make it easier to use.

Reviewing your model

You should have created a basic working model for the youth group leaders. Now it's time to think about whether the model can be improved.

Task 1

Open **Resource 4.3 Modelling questions**. Look at the model you created in Unit 4.2. Answer the following questions:

1. Is it easy to see at a glance which holiday provider offers the best value?
2. Is it clear to the user which variables they can change in order to ask some 'What if…' questions?
3. Is it easy for the user to change those variables if they are not an expert at spreadsheets like you?
4. Would it be easy to use the model to compare value for money across different group sizes?
5. If the answer to any of the questions above is No, suggest ways of improving the model.

Looks matter

The way that data is going to be entered into a model is an important fact for the layout of the document. If the data will be transferred automatically into the model as in Module 1, then the appearance is not so important, although the correct formatting of the cells still is. If the data is to be input by a user, then the appearance and ease of use is very important.

Task 2

Look at **Resource 4.3 Trip 3**.

1. Click on the **Workings** tab at the bottom of the screen. This shows how the model is set up.
2. Now click on the **Choices** tab. This is the same model as on the **Workings** tab, but it has been made much easier for the user.
3. Write down three ways in which the model has been made easier to use.

121

Unit 4.3

Drop-down lists

The use of a **drop-down lists** can speed up data entry. The list will contain only the selections available for the user to enter. This stops incorrect data being entered. Using a selection from a given list like this is one way of ensuring data validation.

Drop-down lists are set up by using the **Data validation** settings and choosing to allow the data to come from a list.

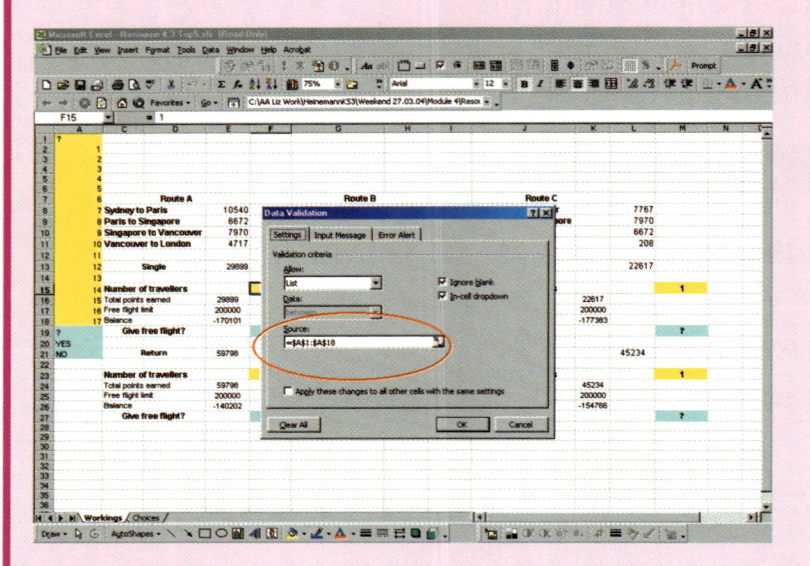

This spreadsheet shows where the data for the list is selected.

A list could contain text or numerical data. It is a sure way of getting a user to enter the type of data that is needed in the cell to make a formula work.

Although a list could be very long, that would not be very sensible if the idea is to speed things up. Sometimes the lists contain just a couple of items – perhaps YES and NO, or Mr, Mrs, Ms, Miss and Other.

Task 3

Open **Resource 4.3 Lists**.

1. There are several data entry boxes. When you click on them to enter data, an arrow appears with a drop down list. Can you see where the data in the lists have come from within the worksheet?

2. Close **Resource 4.3 Lists**.

3. Now open your Holidaysmodel.xls file from Unit 4.2. You are going to create drop-down lists for 'No. of children' in each of the two models.

4. Create a data list for numbers of individual children (1–9) and another list for children in a group (1 to 20).

5. Make cells **E2** and **J2** into drop-down lists using the data lists you have just created.

6. Make any changes to the look of the model, for example background colour, bold, fonts, etc. to make it clear to the user which variables they can change.

7. Save your file as Holidaysmodelv2.xls and close it.

▶ **Skills help**

Creating drop-down lists, page 133.

Editing a chart

The way a chart is displayed can be changed using the **Chart editing** menu. This menu appears if you right mouse click on the chart in the spreadsheet.

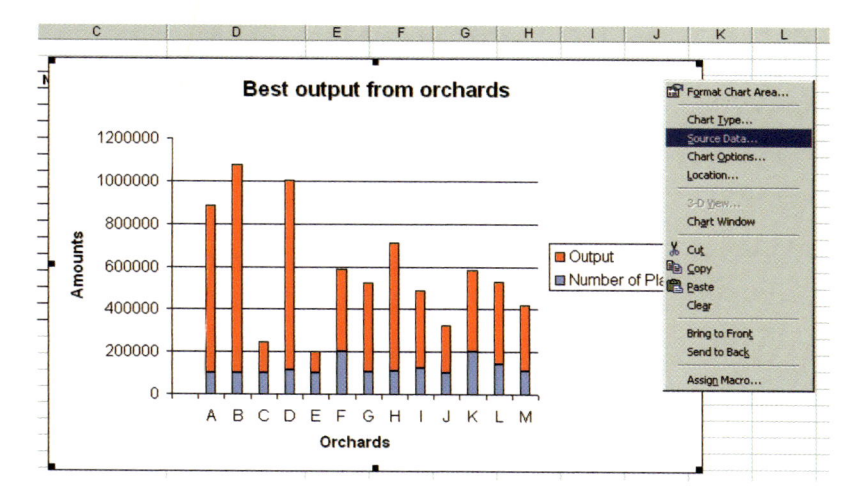

The chart editing menu allows you to alter the way the data has been charted, the way the chart looks, and the chart titles and labels.

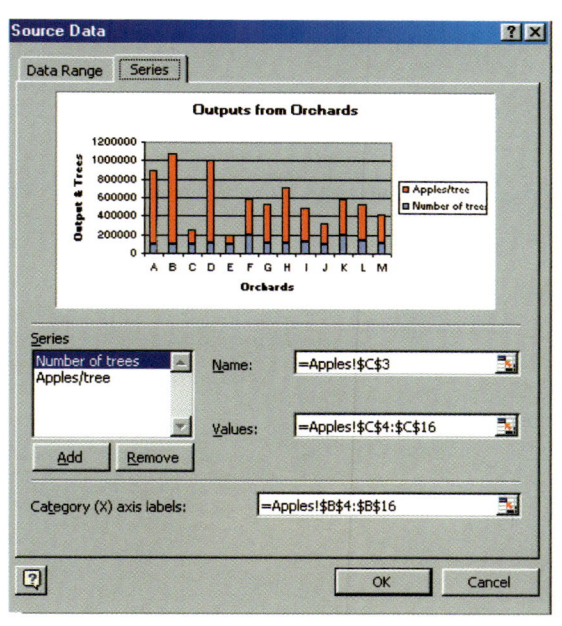

With 'Number of trees' selected in the **Series** box, clicking the **Remove** button will preview the chart with the plot of the 'Number of trees' removed. Clicking **OK** will create the new chart.

Task 4

Open **Resource 4.3 Chart 1**.

1. Use the chart editing facility to create a chart displaying distances from Singapore to the other cities.

Open **Resource 4.3 Chart 2**.

2. Edit this chart to display distances from Singapore.

3. Was it worth editing the charts or would it have been quicker to produce new ones?

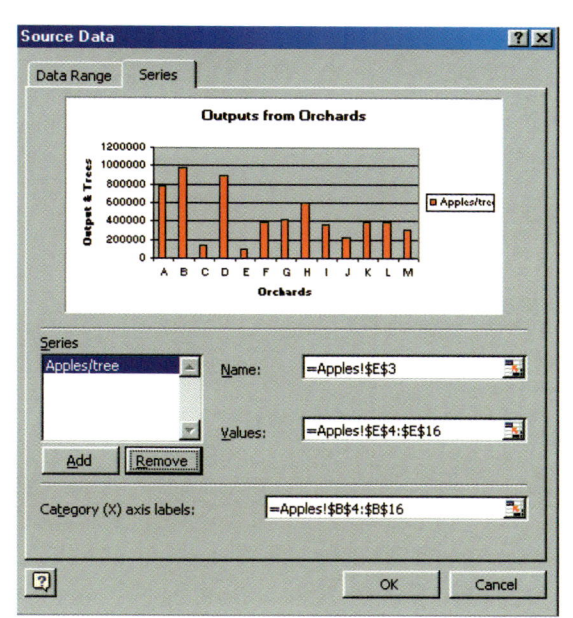

▶ Skills help

Editing charts, page 134.

Unit 4.3

Random numbers

Some models have to allow for a wider range of numbers than those that can be put into a list. The range of the numbers that appears in the list is important, but the model needs to be able to work when any number from the list is used.

For example, suppose you are creating a model about the cost of air travel. Firstly, people have to get to the airport. In the model the distance from the traveller's home to the airport is going to be between 5 and 200 miles. So the journey to the airport can be any value between 5 and 200 (miles).

A **random number generator** model can be set up to generate numbers giving random values within a range. In MS Excel the function used is **=RANDBETWEEN(*,*)**. The * are replaced by the numbers, so this would be =RANDBETWEEN(5,200).

▶ Skills help

Using random numbers, pages 135–136.

Task 5

Open **Resource 4.3 Random**.

1. Click on cells between **C8** and **C17**. A formula has been used to generate the values.

2. The graph shows the mileage for a random sample of ten people who all live between 5 and 200 miles from the airport.

3. Press the **<F9>** key to generate more random numbers. What happens to the chart?

4. Close this file and open your Holidaysmodelv2.xls file from Unit 4.3. Save a different version of it under the file name Holidaysmodelv3.xls.

5. In the new version, remove the drop down lists in cells **E2** and **J2**.

6. You are going to type formulae to generate random numbers in cells **E2** and **J2**. The function you need is **=RANDBETWEEN (*,*)**. What should the numbers in the formula be?

7. Type the random number function into cells **E2** and **J2**.

8. Press **<F9>** a few times. What happens to the numbers?

9. Save the file and exit.

Extending and improving a model

Case study

The youth leaders would like to be able to compare prices for a range of numbers of children, from 2–20. In order to do this you will need to extend and amend your model, so that you can show costs for different numbers of children at the same time.

Unit 4.3

Module Task

Open **Resource 4.3 Holidays 3**. Save it as Holidaysmodelv4.xls.

You will see that the data has been rearranged so that there are now a number of columns to the right of the model each with a number in it. These are the numbers of children.

The formulae that go in the columns underneath need to include all the calculations needed to produce the total cost of sending that number of children on holiday.

1. Write down the formula that you think needs to go in cell **F3**. Check it by using your old Holidays model (Holidaysmodel.xls) and entering 2 in the number of children for individual bookings. Did you get the same answer?

2. Remember you are going to be copying and pasting these formulae. Do you need to use any absolute cell references? If so, add these now.

3. Copy and paste the formula from **F3** into the rest of the cells in column **F**. Do the answers look sensible? If they do, then copy and paste the formulae across columns **G** to **I**. Check the results.

4. The formula for cell **J3** is more complicated because it needs to include the group discount. Use the **Skills help** and work with a partner to decide what this formula should be.

5. When you are happy that you have got it right, add any absolute cell references you need, and then copy and paste the formula down column **J**. Then copy and paste the formula across columns **K** to **O**.

6. Create a line graph that will display the outputs of the models. Some of the lines are very close together. Experiment with altering the scale of the Y axis. Can you make it clearer?

7. Try creating separate graphs for individual bookings and group bookings.

8. Write down which holiday provider gives the best value for groups of 4, 10, 16 and 20 children.

9. Save and close your file.

▶ Skills help

Writing formulae, pages 134–135.
Resource 4.2 Formulae.

Unit 4.3

Models and simulations everywhere

You have created models using a spreadsheet. You have used a model to simulate what could happen in a real-life situation, and to ask 'What if' questions.

There are many other ways of creating models and simulations using ICT. You may have used some in other lessons such as Design and Technology, Science or Geography. You have almost certainly used other types of models and simulations at home and with your friends.

Task 6

Make a list of other types of ICT models or simulations you can think of.

Here are a couple of clues:
- Walt Disney
- Bookings.

- A simulation can look quite lifelike.
- A model might not be visible, but could be set up to work in the background.

Test centre

1. What is a drop-down menu?
2. What is a random number generator?
3. What is meant by a computer model?

Unit 4.4
Simulations and models

In this unit you are going to discover how models and simulations are used on the Internet. You will also look at some of the ways that databases are used through websites and how data can be protected.

Models and simulations

A model is a set of instructions that represents a real-world event or object. Models can be created on a computer using many different programs, including spreadsheets.

A simulation is what happens when you run a computer model. Sometimes this simply means displaying the results of a 'What if …?' query in a spreadsheet. Other simulations are very complex. For example, a computer football game is a simulation. It is based on a model that represents what happens in a real football game.

All simulations are based on a model. In a computer game the model is called a 'black box' model because you cannot see it. All the graphic action that you see on the screen is controlled by the instructions in the black box model. The inputs are the clicks you make, and the outputs are the moves of the players and the ball on the screen.

Unit 4.4

Task 1

Look at the four websites that make use of models, which can be found at:

http://www.heinemann.co.uk/hotlinks

What is the difference between the types of model that are used on these websites?

Passwords

When using online games and bookings, the owners of the websites often ask people to register with them. This is so that they can use the information provided by the user in their marketing. It also allows them to make sure that the person who is using the website is really that person.

Some websites will ask you to set up a **password**. Others will ask for your email address and will send you a password to use when you next visit the website.

Which method is the most secure for the user?

Which is the best method for the website owners?

Passwords show up on the screen as a series of * or other graphics, which replace the actual data that is keyed into the computer. This is done to make sure that the password is secure, as no one can see what password has been typed in.

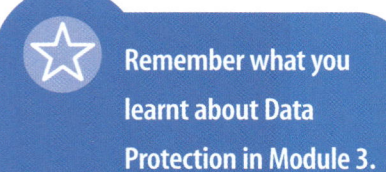

> ★ **Remember what you learnt about Data Protection in Module 3.**

Developers can also use a technique called **encryption** to secure data files. Encryption is a method of scrambling the data so that only people who have the 'key' to unscramble it are able to look at the data. It is just like a code.

Module Task

You need to find out some information about methods of travel to the four countries in your web game. You are going to carry out research into the online booking systems that are available for the countries' airlines.

You will also identify how secure you think your data is when you are looking at the websites.

Use **Resource 4.4 Flights** to record your findings from each of the websites.

1. Open a web browser and look at the four airline websites, which can be found at: http://heinemann.co.uk/hotlinks

2. Look at the way each of the websites has been laid out.
   - Do you need to use your email address?
   - Do you need a password?

3. Make a note of the data that you are asked for when you are finding out the information.

4. Bookmark these websites so you will be able to create a link to them from your web game.

So how do they work?

Behind each of these websites is an enormous database. The database holds all of the information about flights, times, dates, aircraft, luggage allowances and on and on and on.

When data is entered into the online form, the database is searched to see what matches with the data. The results are then output together into a report.

This all starts to sound quite familiar.

Unit 4.4

Task 2

Look at the airline website that you found the easiest to use in the Module task.

1. Make notes about the layout of the web page.
2. Open a spreadsheet program.
3. Set up a model that can take data in the same way as the online booking website, and produce the same output information.

You only need to create the first page as you do not have the database to put behind this first data input screen.

Task 3

You have now collected all of the information that you need to put together your web game.

Before you can start on the game you need to make sure that you have:
- carried out a web query from Module 1
- carried out the development of web pages in Module 2
- carried out searches in Module 3
- carried out an investigation of online models in this unit
- developed a model to input and output data in this unit.

If you have missed out any of these, return to the relevant unit before beginning Module 5.

Test centre

1. Are online games simulations or models?
2. Why do we need passwords?
3. What is encryption and who uses it?

Module 4 Assignment

Souvenirs

A group of people, four from each of the four countries in your web game, is to visit your local community. To complete Module 4 you are going to develop a model to help the organisers of this trip.

Background

The model is meant to help the organisers budget for the visit. They want to give each visitor the same complete package of souvenirs. But if the organisers have not got enough funds to cover this, the model should help them revise their plans.

The organisers want to offer each visitor:
- a book about each of the countries, including their own and the UK
- a music CD from the UK charts, and
- a souvenir tour T-shirt.

Brief

Your model should work out the total cost of providing the full souvenir package, where all the visitors get all the souvenirs.

Your model should also be able to work out what the total cost would be if each visitor was not given a book about their own country, but was given everything else.

Write a report explaining the conclusions you have reached for the organisers.

The cost of the items is shown in the table.

Book about Australia	£6.50
Book about Singapore	£5.75
Book about France	£12.00
Book about Canada	£8.60
Book about UK	£10.50
UK chart CD	£12.00
Tour T-shirt	£5.00

Extension
Other 'What ifs?'

Modify your model or develop new models to allow for the following:

- The UK chart CD is purchased from a website where the price change from week to week. (Hint: set up a web query to a website with prices for CDs).
- Each visitor might not want every souvenir. The visitors should be able to record in the model which souvenirs they want. The model should then calculate the cost.

> ★ Start by working out the layout of the model.
> - What column headings do you need?
> - What formulae will be needed?
> - What should it calculate?
>
> When running your models, estimate what you think the results should be so that you have some idea of whether or not the model is working accurately.

Module 4

Skills help

Adding new entries into a spreadsheet

1. Click in the row below where you would like the new row to appear.
2. Click on **Insert**, **Rows**.
3. A new row will appear. Type in the new data.

Trial and improvement and Goal Seek

Using trial and Improvement

You can use Trial and Improvement to find out how many trips have to be made between Singapore and Vancouver to be able to claim a free flight, if a free flight needs 35,000 miles to have been flown. Increase the number of trips by 1 in cell **B8** until the total distance travelled to or from Vancouver in cell **H8** becomes greater than 35,000.

Or you can estimate what the number of trips might be and try that.

This example shows that an estimate of five trips will be more than 35,000 miles, but you still need to check out four trips, just in case four trips would also give more than 35,000.

Entering four trips in cell **B8** shows that it is under 35,000, so the answer is definitely five trips.

These numbers are not too bad to have to use Trial and Improvement for, but it would be more difficult using this method for trips between London and Paris!

Using Goal Seek

The software has a tool that can be used for carrying out the same process called Goal Seek. In this example the free flights at 35,000 miles are going to be earned between London and Paris

1. Click in cell **F9**, the cell that holds the target value of the total distance travelled to or from Paris.
2. Go to the **Tools** menu, select **Goal Seek** and the **Goal Seek** dialogue box will open.

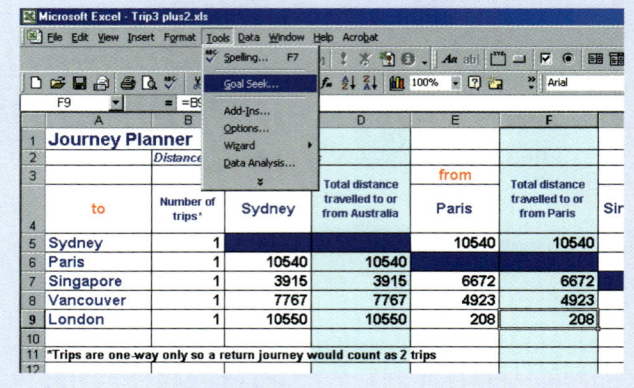

3. In the **To value** box enter **35,000**. This is the Target value that we are trying to hit in cell **F9**. Click in the **Set cell** box, and then click in cell **F9** to enter the cell reference needed.

4 In the **By changing cell** box enter **$B$9**. It is the value in cell **B9** - What 'Number of trips' between London and Paris, will make the total distance travelled to or from Paris greater than 35,000 miles, that we want the software to calculate for us.

5 Click in the **By changing cell** box, and then click in cell **B9** to enter the cell reference needed.

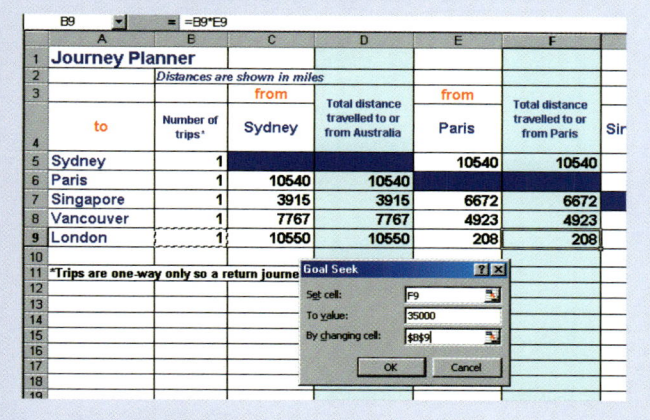

6 Click **OK** and the answer is returned.

Goal Seek actually tells us that 168.269 trips give a total distance travelled of 35,000 miles. So 169 trips would be needed to travel further than the 35,000 mile target.

7 Click **OK** to close the **Goal Seek Status** dialogue box.

Creating drop down lists

1 Click in a cell and select **Data** from the menu bar.

2 Click on **Validation** and the **Data Validation** dialogue box will open.

3 Select **List** from the drop down list in the **Allow** box.

4 Click in the **Source** box and then click and drag cells to give the cell references of the list of values you want to appear in your drop down list.

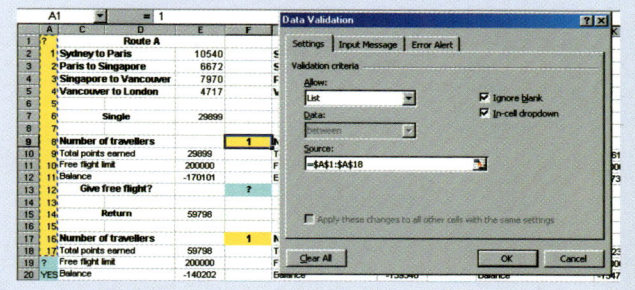

5 Click **OK**.

6 The drop down list is created and can be displayed by clicking on the arrow in the datasheet.

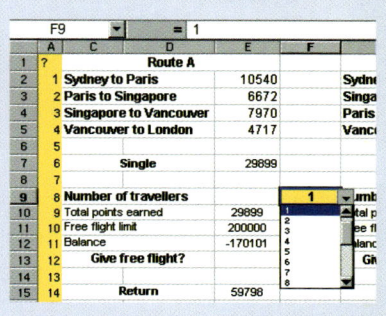

7 If you do not want the list to be visible make the font colour the same as the background colour using **Format**, **Cells** from the menu bar.

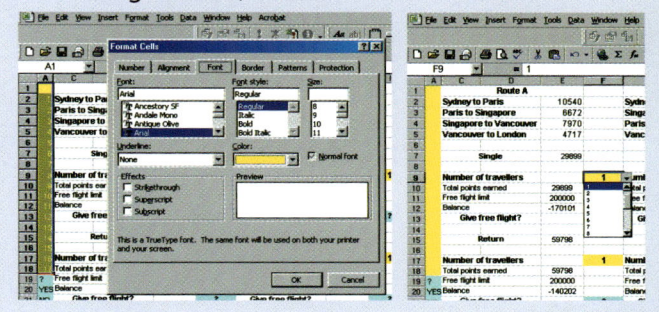

Editing charts

Changing the data source in charts

The chart showing distances from Paris to the other cities needs to be edited to create a chart showing distances from Vancouver instead.

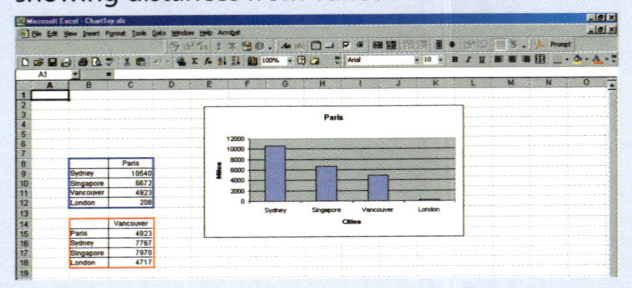

1 Right mouse click on the chart.
2 Select **Source Data** from the menu. The **Source Data** dialogue box will open. This allows you to edit the data on which the chart is based.

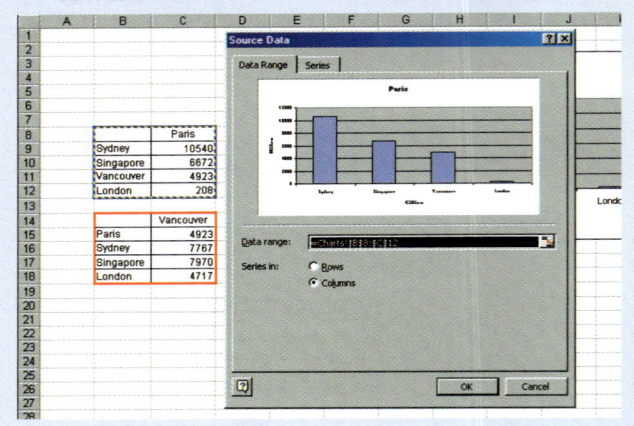

The **Data range** box shows the cells being used in the chart are cells B8:C12. These are the cells outlined in blue. Absolute cell references are being used.

The chart needs to show the data shown in the red table instead.

3 The contents of the **Data range** box are already selected when the dialogue box opens.
Click in cell **B14** and drag across to cell **C18** to enter the data range of the red table in to the box.

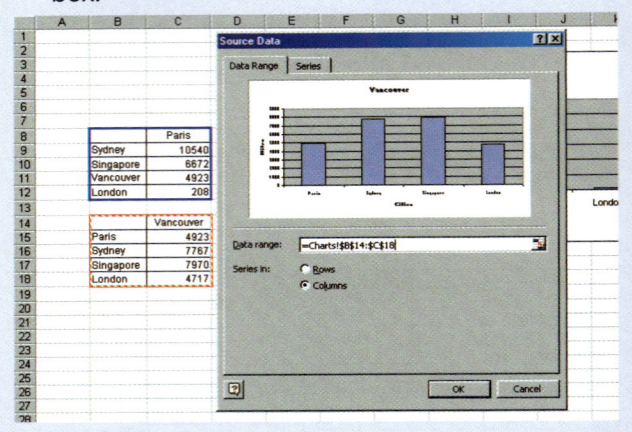

4 Click **OK**.

The edited chart is displayed.

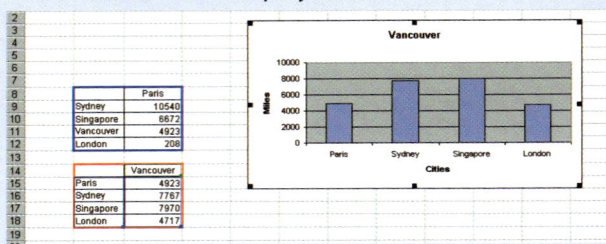

Writing formulae

The basics

All formulae begin with =.

Formulae are typed in the cell in which you want the answer to appear.

You can use cell references in formulae, for example =B2+C2 adds up the numbers in cells **B2** and **C2**.

The signs used in formulae are:

+ for plus
- for minus
* for multiply
/ for divide

Using brackets in formulae

If a calculation is complex you sometimes need to group bits of it together to make it work properly. This is done by using brackets.

=(4+4+4)/2 is a complex calculation. It adds up a series of numbers (4+4+4) and then divides the result by 2. The answer is 6.

Putting the brackets in the right place is important. Without the brackets, only the last number in the series is divided by 2 and the answer is 10.

Cell references

Relative cell referencing

If you copy a formula using either copy and paste or the fill handle, the software will automatically adjust the cell references within the formula to the new position.

| =D15+E15+F15+G15+H15+I15 |
| =D16+E16+F16+G16+H16+I16 |

Absolute cell referencing

Sometimes we do not want the computer to adjust the cell references when we copy a formula. The way to stop it is to type $ in front of *both bits* of the cell reference, i.e. in front of the letter *and* the number: e.g. **$B$2**.

| =D15+E15+F15+G15+$H$15 |
| =D16+E16+F16+G16+$H$15 |

Absolute cell referencing is useful if you have one particular piece of fixed information, for example a price, which you want to keep referring to in lots of different formulae.

$E$5 is the absolute cell reference for cell **E5**, shown in red in the spreadsheet.

The value that is placed in cell **E5** will then appear anywhere else in the spreadsheet, or will be used in formulae if the absolute cell reference is used.

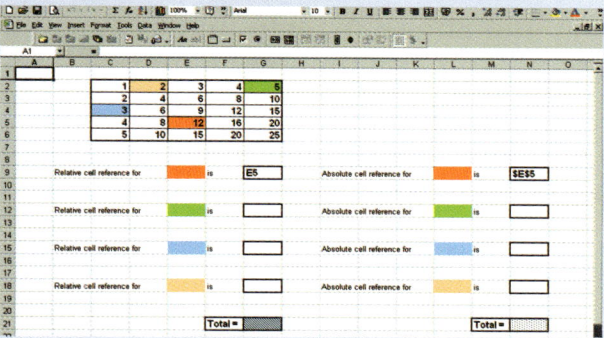

Using random numbers

To set up a model that can use any number from within a given range the **RANDBETWEEN(*,*)** function is used. The * are replaced with the numbers at each end of the range.

For example if a group of 20 people live within a range of 50 – 350 miles of an airport **RANDBETWEEN(50,350)** could be used to create a value anywhere between 50 and 350.

1 Enter the function in the top cell of the column where the random numbers should appear, **C5** in this case.

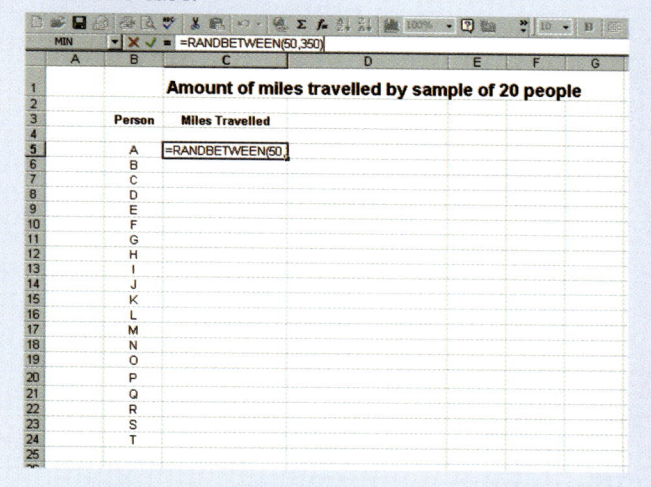

2 Left click and drag from **C5** to **C24** to highlight the cells.

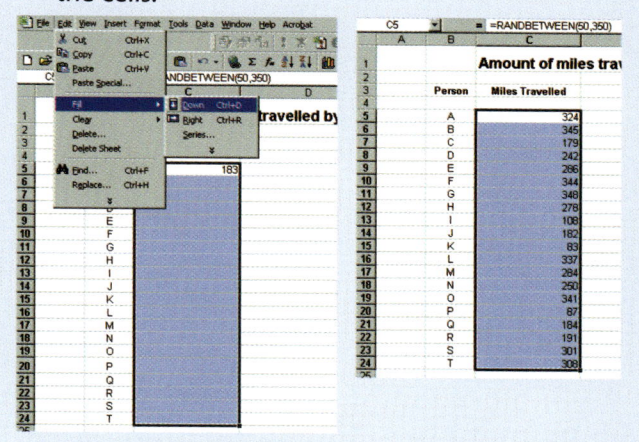

3 Go to **Edit**, select **Fill**.
4 Click **Down**, this is used to copy the function in the remaining 19 cells.

Skills 4

5 Highlight the cells **B3:C24**.

6 Use the **Chart wizard** to create a chart from the data.

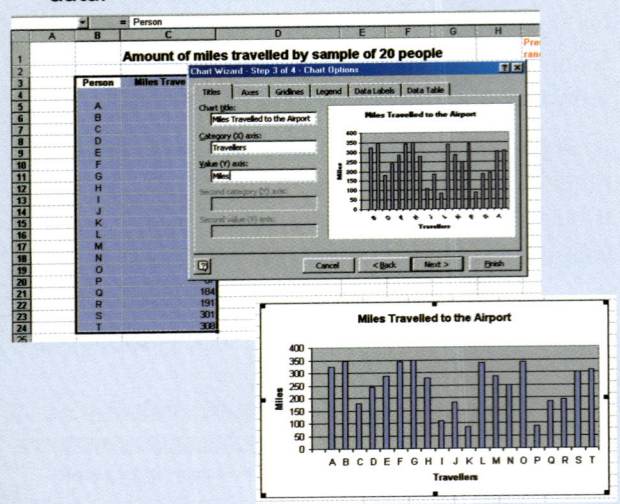

7 Press **<F9>** to get a different set of random numbers generated and charted.

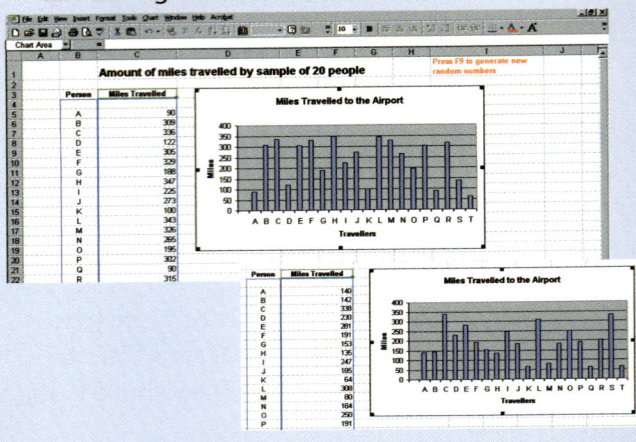

Module 5
An ICT system

Learning Targets

In this module your are going to develop an ICT system – your website game. You are going to use the information that you gathered in Modules 1–4 and put it all together into the web game.

The game will be based around your characters from four countries:
- Australia
- France
- Canada
- Singapore

You will learn about the life cycle of an ICT system and the stages involved in its development.

In Module 5 you are going to learn:

About the life cycle of a system	See page 141
How to carry out a feasibility study for your web game	See page 141
How to plan out the way the website will work	See pages 142–146
How to create a model to help work out the cost of developing the web game	See page 147
How to draw a structure diagram for your website	See page 145
How to create a website	See pages 149–150
How controls can be added into a website	See pages 152–155
How to use and create mimics for use on your website	See pages 156–157
How to create a simple control program	See pages 159–160
How to work out the best way to market the website and produce a 'marketing package' for a target audience	See pages 161–167
How to write an evaluation report and analyse what you have done	See pages 169–170

You will also collect together all of the information for the different sections of your web game from things you did in Modules 1–4.

What are your targets for this module?

To achieve a level 4 in this module you will need to *level 4*
- Work out what needs to be in the website to meet the audience's needs
- Prepare web pages and, with support, work out how they will link together
- Use hyperlinks to link the web pages together

Learning Targets 5

- Describe the rules and enter numbers and formulae into a spreadsheet model to work out whether the budget will cover the cost of developing the web game
- Check your formulae and change some variables to try out various possible outcomes
- Identify how the use of control features could improve your website
- Plan and create a simple program to control output channels in a seven line matrix in order to display the numbers 0–9. This could be used to create a countdown timer for your web game
- Test your program by changing the input and output channels to display each number in turn
- Combine text and images to create marketing materials to tell the target audience about your website. Carry out a mail merge on pre-prepared data with assistance
- Use some given criteria to write an evaluation report about your web game

To achieve a level 5 in this module you will need to   *level 5*
- Write a feasibility study and development plan for your web game
- Design and create web pages that will be suitable for the target audience, and decide on the best way to link them together to make the game work properly
- Use hyperlinks to link the web pages in the way that is most effective for the audience, and explain why you did it the way you did
- Work out the inputs and rules for a spreadsheet model to decide whether the budget will cover the cost of developing the web game. Enter the formulae required, using absolute cell references if necessary
- Add more variables to make the model more realistic. Use the model to decide whether the web game development is feasible within the budget allowed. Present your conclusions using charts and graphs
- Identify how the use of control features could improve your website, saying what types of inputs and outputs might be needed
- Plan and create a program to control output channels in a seven line matrix in order to display the numbers 0–9 in reverse sequence at the press of a single button. Test your program
- Write and run a program to test a six page mimic. Check that each page of the mimic works by changing the input and output channels in the program
- Combine and refine text and images to create a range of different marketing materials to tell the target audience about your website. Design and create a suitable customer database file and run a mail merge with assistance
- Develop criteria for evaluating your own and other people's web games. Make improvements to your web game as a result of your evaluation

To achieve a level 6 in this module you will need to   *level 6*
- Prepare a feasibility study for your website which covers all aspects of the project and presents your conclusions clearly and appropriately for the target audience
- Plan and create the best web game for your audience, breaking the job down into a series of small tasks
- Make use of ICT tools wherever possible to automate procedures and ensure that your web game works efficiently
- Develop a spreadsheet model to work out whether the budget will cover the cost of developing the web game. Use efficient methods of testing predictions such as Goal Seek
- Add new variables and rules to improve your model. Check the validity of your conclusions by looking at information from other sources
- Create some control features and integrate them into your web game to make it more interactive
- Plan and create your own six page mimic, setting an output channel for each page of the mimic
- Write and run a program to test your mimic. Check that each page of your mimic works by changing the input and output channels. Use your own ideas to improve them so that they work more efficiently
- Use automated procedures such as mail merge as part of your marketing campaign for the web game. Make improvements to your marketing materials as a result of feedback from the target audience
- Test and refine your web game by collecting feedback from a range of users in your school, possibly by creating a response form on your website

Learning Targets 5

What do you know already?

System

A system is something that requires an **input**, **process** and **output** to happen.

Input. The stage where the system receives an external signal to make something happen, for example a signal from a sensor.

Process. The stage where decisions are made based on the input, for example it might be a calculation, or a move between pages in a website.

Output. The stage where something happens as a result of the process, this could be a chart being updated or a window closing.

Life cycle of a system

A system is always changing. The development of a system goes through a number of stages, with each stage having an impact on the system. Perhaps it is right at the start when the system is first being created, or perhaps it is when it is being used and might need updating. The stages of the life cycle are:

- **Identify and analyse**
- **Design**
- **Implement**
- **Test**
- **Evaluate**

Identify and analyse. Identify how the system will work, the input, process and ouput. Analyse what the user will expect, and what the system will do and will not do.

Design. Plan the system, developing the input, process and output parts of the system so that they work together.

Implement. Create the system from the design.

Test. Make sure the system works using test criteria, and that it does what it is meant to do by checking it against the analysis.

Evaluate. Assess how the system is working and make any necessary improvements. This stage also involves maintaining the system so that it continues to work well.

Learning Targets 5

Sequencing events.

To make sure that things happen in the correct order, the sequence of events that make up the system have to be put into the right order. This is called sequencing events. Drawing a **flowchart** is often helpful.

Flowcharts. These are one way of showing the sequence of events in the correct order. Flowcharts also show the input, process and output stages of the system.

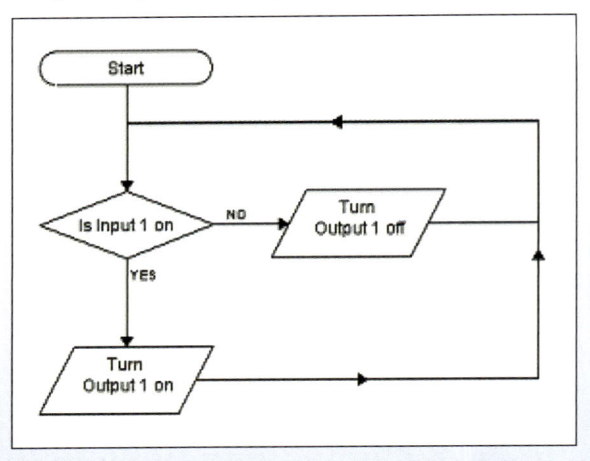

Computer systems

A computer system is made up of a computer, its software and all the equipment attached to the computer. So there is the input equipment such as the keyboard, mouse and scanner; the process equipment, which involves the computer and all the software needed; and the output equipment such as the monitor, printer and speakers.

Task

Open **Resource 5 Systems**. For each of the systems in the table state what you think happens at the input, process and output stages.

Unit 5.1
Planning a system

In this unit you will learn about the life cycle of a system and the stages of development needed for a system.

Life cycle of a system

What does the word cycle make you think about…round, revolving, a circle? A system can be planned in stages that complete a circle, or cycle. The diagram shows a simple **system life cycle**.

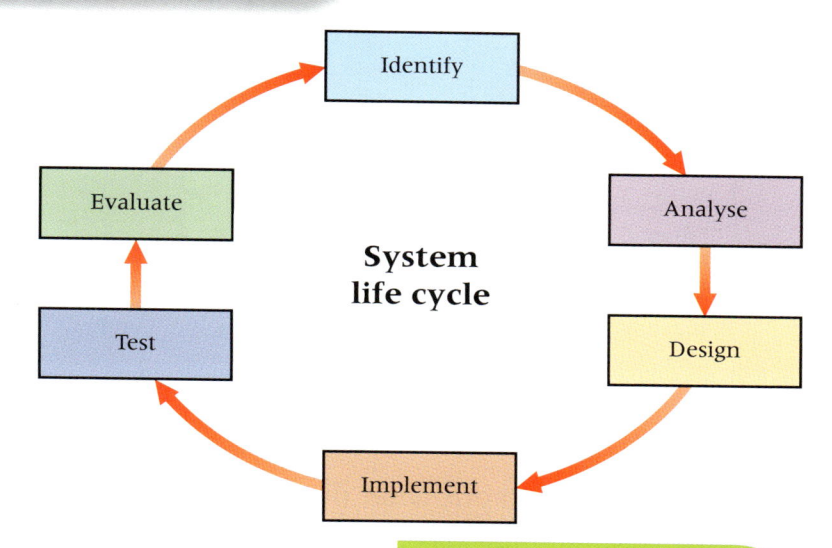

System life cycle: Identify → Analyse → Design → Implement → Test → Evaluate

Identify

A stage in a system's development where it is identified by whom, where and when a system might be needed or used.

Feasibility study

Before work can begin on developing a system, you need to determine whether it is worth developing in the first place. A feasibility study needs to be carried out, asking questions like:

- Is a system needed?
- What would the purpose of the system be?
- How would it be developed?
- Who would use it?
- Can it be developed within the budget?

Answers to these questions help you to make decisions about the structure of a system, and how big and complex it should be.

Task 1

Open **Resource 5.1 Feasibility study**.

1. Using the points listed on the left as a guide, write down some questions that could be used in a feasibility study about your web based game. Remind yourself of the specification of the game by looking again at **Resource Specification**.

2. Alongside each question, list the group or the individuals (people with particular knowledge and skills) who should be asked the questions. Think about such things as
   - who is the audience for the game?
   - who should you ask about development?
   - who should you ask about budgets?

141

Unit 5.1

PLEASE HELP!

We need an interesting section on the community website that will make people of your age want to look at the website.

We want a simple game that users could have fun with and that show links between our community and four other countries that we have links with:

- Australia
- Canada
- France
- Singapore

Development plan

Once you have found out what the users need in a game, the development has to be planned in stages.

The development plan needs to include details of:

- functions – what the different bits will do
- layout – what all the different bits will look like
- resources – what the content is and where it will come from (text, images)

The development plan should also:

- ensure that things are developed in the right order. (One aspect of the system might depend on another having already been completed)
- establish how the system will be tested
- list the criteria to be used in testing the system
- state who will test the system.

Module Task

Use a table like this one to make a list of all of the different features that will have to be developed or found before the whole of the game comes together.

The first aspect has been completed so that you can see the type of detail that you need to put into your plan.

Item	Comments
Navigation	Structure of the website, how the user will be able to move around the website.
Web page style	Look and feel for all web pages. Some work already done in Module 2.
Web page content	List of what will appear on each page. Some work already done.

Add more rows as needed.

Timeline

A development plan needs to identify in which order the stages will be carried out. This means that you need to prioritise the features in order of importance. For example, you need to know how the website will be navigated before you can plan what navigation buttons you need.

The development plan therefore needs to include a timeline, which outlines when each stage of development will be carried out. The time line is like a production line in a factory, with the product made in stages.

Unit 5.1

Task 2

Create a timeline showing the stages of development need to make sure that the website is produced efficiently.

▶ **Skills help**

Creating a timeline for development, page 173.

Task 3

1 Look at the character web pages and the web game structure diagram that you created in Module 2, check them against the features list you created in the Module task. (The web pages should be stored in the Web game website XX and YY *folder you created in Unit 2.6*).

2 Make a note of any features on your pages that are not in your list?

3 Correct your list if you discover there are features missing from it.

Test centre

1 What is meant by the life cycle of system?
2 What is a feasibility study?
3 Why is a development plan important?

Unit 5.2
Modelling a system

In this unit you are going to analyse what your system should do and develop the structure of the web game. You will also use a spreadsheet model to consider the costs of developing the game.

Analyse

In, out and what?

In the same way as with any system, a web game will need input, process and output stages.

The **INPUT** will be the clicks that the user makes to navigate around the website.

The **PROCESS** will be the hyperlinks set up between the different pages or external data.

The **OUTPUT** will be the screen that appears as a result of the process.

Sample web game

The structure, and therefore the model of the system, will be set by what the INPUT, PROCESS and OUTPUT stages are meant to do.

The complicated diagram on the next page shows a possible structure for the game with one mystery guest.

An **INPUT** click is indicated by the 'input' end of a hyperlink being shown in **RED**.

A **PROCESS** is indicated by the 'destination' end of a hyperlink being shown in **BLUE**.

An **OUTPUT** is shown in **GREEN**.

A web page is shown like this:

A data file is shown like this:

Task 1

First plan a storyline through your game. This is your analysis of what the system will do.

Use the structure diagram that you created in Unit 2.6.

1. Imagine clicking the hyperlinks or buttons. Follow the arrows around the site as you imagine visiting the web pages, reading the clues, giving answers and getting responses from the system.

2. Use **Resource 5.2 Walk through** to record what happens on each web page.

3. Repeat steps 1 and 2 using the sample web game shown on the next page.

145

Unit 5.2

Structure diagram

Community Home Page
Young People Section

Young People Home Page
Click here to go to our new web game

Web Game Home Page
Click on the Mystery Guest for clues to help you guess where they are from

Mystery Guest Image

Fact File 1 Spreadsheet — back
Fact File 2 Character Web pages — back
Fact File 3 Database — back
Fact File 4 Spreadsheet — back

Click for help in solving clues from:
- Fact File music
- Fact file Mystery Guest
- Fact File country life
- Fact File distances

Clues Page
- Music clue
- Guest clue
- Country life clue
- Distances clue

Ready to answer? — Home

Ready to answer?
Mystery Guest from
- Australia
- France
- Canada
- Singapore
Chose & click box

Correct Answer
Congratulations!!
Home

Incorrect Answer
Sorry but that's wrong
Try Again — Home

Task 2

1. Now you have walked through and have storylines for your own web game and the sample web game, identify and record any problems with your website.

2. Redesign your web game to overcome these problems. Keep a note of what changes you make and why.

3. Create a final, accurate structure diagram for your redesigned web game.

▶ Skills help

For an example of a completed Resource analysis sheet table for the content of the website game look at **Resource 5.2 Web analysis**.

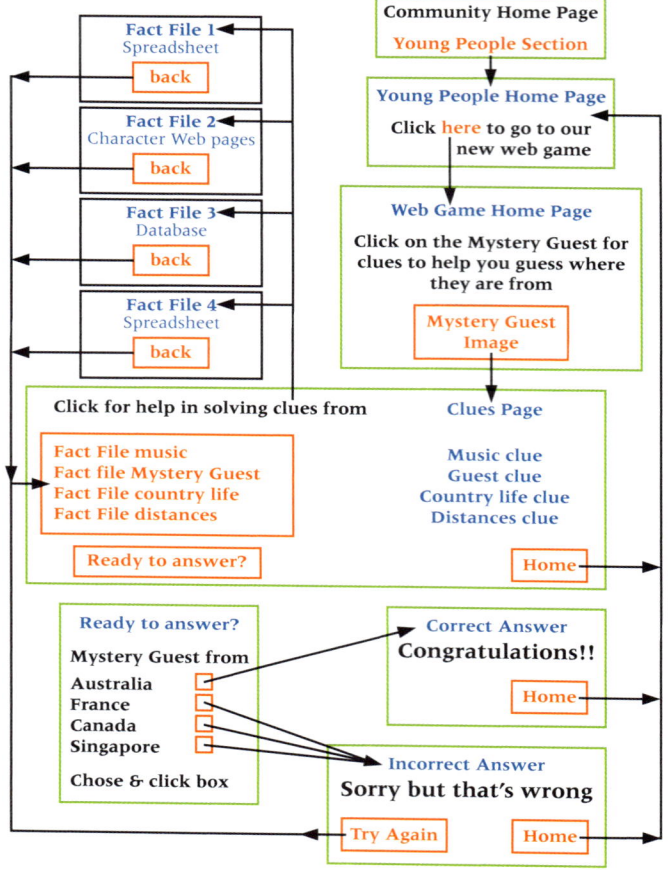

Resources

Completing a Web analysis sheet will help your understanding of the web game and, by listing the components, it will help you see what is still needed.

Task 3

🖱 Open **Resource 5.2 Web analysis 1**.

Page name	Text	Image	Navigation		Description	Log
			Button	Hyperlink		
Community home page	T1				Community home page	
				L1	Young people's section	
Young people's home page	T2				Young people's home page. Click (here) to go to our new web game	

1. Use your latest structure diagram from Task 2 to complete the table showing all the components of your web game. Take care not to list the same item more than once, even if you need to use it again. For example, the same home page button could appear on several web pages.

2. The next stage is to identify the items and content that you still need to create. Tick the components you have got in the Log column, and leave blank the ones that you still need to create or locate.

Unit 5.2

> ⭐ **Remember:** Any of the web pages from Module 2 that you are going to adapt for use in the web game need to be copied from the *Character Website* folder into the *Web game website XX and YY* folder itself.

Cost

The development of a website can be very expensive. The people developing a website will charge for the development of the design and content for each web page, and for creating the navigation of the website itself.

To work out the cost of developing a website and therefore whether it is affordable, a model can be created that will calculate the costs.

Module Task

Create a spreadsheet model that will calculate the cost of developing the website for **one** mystery guest.

Your model must show the effect on the cost of the website of changing the number of:

- text items
- images
- buttons
- hyperlinks
- web pages.

The website that you are going to develop has the following costs:

Component of the website	Cost per item
Text items	£100 per page
Images	£50 per image
Buttons	£25 per button design
Hyperlinks	£25 per hyperlink
Web page design	£250 per page
Website structure design fee	£600
Management fee	30% of total

Open **Resource 5.2 Web analysis 2**.

1. Use the list you created in Task 3 to complete the Total number required column for each of the website components.

One mystery guest	
Components	Total number required
Text items	
Images	
Buttons	
Hyperlinks	
Web pages	

2. Create the spreadsheet model.

3. Develop the model so that it checks to see whether the website is within the allocated budget of £5250.

147

Unit 5.2

Task 4

Extra mystery guests could be introduced to the game, so long as it falls within the allocated budget. A player would then choose one of the mystery guests and try to work out where they are from, as before.

1. Work out the impact on the web game of having **two** mystery guests. Sketch out those parts of the structure diagram that have changed.

2. Open **Resource 5.2 Web analysis 2** again and complete the table for a game with two mystery guests.

3. Work out the impact on the web game of having **three** mystery guests. Sketch out those parts of the structure diagram that have changed and complete the table on **Resource 5.2 Web analysis 2** for three mystery guests.

4. Look out for patterns that are emerging. For example, how many extra pages are needed each time there is an extra mystery guest added to the web game?

5. Create a spreadsheet model that will allow the cost of developing the website to be calculated for different numbers of mystery guests.

Test centre

1. List the stages in the life cycle of a system.
2. What do you need to do during the analysis stage of the life cycle?
3. What does a structure diagram show you?

Unit 5.3
Developing a system

In this unit you are going to design and create the web pages needed to make up your web game. Working with a partner you will each create some of the website, evaluating each other's work as you progress.

Design

The web pages can be designed in any of the ways that you found out about in Module 2. The most straightforward way to create web pages is to use web design software, such as MS FrontPage.

It is important to use the same layout for the web pages. The contents will vary from page to page, but with the same layout on each page, the user should soon learn where to click to successfully navigate around the site.

Remind yourself of how the web design software you are going to use works.

Remember
You must store all the web pages, images and data files for the website in the same folder. This folder is your *Web game website XX and YY* folder. If all of the files are not in the same folder the website will not function correctly.

IT IS IMPORTANT THAT ALL FILES ARE IN THE SAME FOLDER. THAT MEANS IMAGES AS WELL!

Task 1

1. Working with your partner, open the web pages from your Character Website *folder that you think might be useful in the web game website.*

2. Discuss whether one of your existing web page layouts would work for the web game, either as it stands or with some modification. You may decide a new layout would be best.

3. Adapt your chosen layout or create a new one ready for use in the web game.

4. Together, examine your data files and decide which you will use in the game. Do you need to make any improvements to these data files?

Unit 5.3

Sharing out the development tasks

To make efficient progress you need to share the work out between you and your partner. You need to decide who will:
- finalise the layout of the web pages
- finalise the design of the buttons
- think up the clues
- gather together the resources – images, text items and buttons
- check that all the files open properly.

Devising clues

You need to design the clues so that a user playing the game can get help to solve them by looking at a data file or a fact file web page.

For example the following clue could be based on the information in the characters database you created in Module 3.

Our mystery guest can leave school at 16.

You need to create a bank of clues based on your work in Modules 1, 2, 3 and 4. There should be clues from each module. Remember your fact files covered:
- local music (Module 1)
- your characters, what they look like, where they live, and what they like (Module 2)
- life in the four countries (Module 3)
- the distances between the capital cities of the countries (Module 4).

Task 2

Open **Resource 5.2 Web Analysis 1** again.

1. Check through the items listed in **Resource 5.2 Web Analysis 1** that still need to be created or located and put your initials in the **Log** column to record who is doing what.

   Remember there could be items in your character web pages that could be re-used or adapted.

2. Are any of the items dependent on another one being finished first? If so, what are you going to do to ensure this does not stop the development?

3. Decide who is going to review which data files.

4. You should both create clues and decide later which to use. Open **Resource 5.3 Clues** and list the clues as you come up with them.

Unit 5.3

Module Task

Get on and do the work you set out in Task 2.

Something to consider:
When a player has looked at the fact files they need to return to the clues page. If you expect them to use the **Back** button to do this, you will need to tell them this. You also need to decide where you will tell them this.

You will not be able to have all the hyperlinks actively working until you have created the web pages that these will take you to. Decide how to manage this aspect of the design. There are two options:
- Are you going to wait and make them live when all the web pages have been designed?
- Are you going to put them in place and only see if they work when the other pages have been developed?

What problems could arise with either of these methods?

▶ **Skills help**

Developing web pages, pages 63–69 module 2.

Task 3

Open **Resource 5.3 Check out**.

1 As you are developing the web game components, check out each other's work and make comments on how they could improve them.

Open **Resource 5.3 Website testing**.

2 Get others in the class to test your website, record their comments and the improvements you made to your website as a result.

Test centre

1 Why do you need to store all the files for your web game in one folder?
2 Why is it important to plan the development in stages?
3 What could be a problem with hyperlinks during development?

151

Unit 5.4
Using control systems to automate a process

In this unit you are going to learn about systems that use sequential control and those that respond to user interaction. You will write a program to demonstrate an interactive control system.

Methods of control

The method of control can vary, it could be voice activated, a touch screen, or more traditionally through a joystick, mouse or keyboard. Although input devices often differ in shape and colour they all do basically the same thing.

Some input devices allow the user to turn switches either on or off, these are called digital devices. While other input devices, like a slider or light sensor, have a number of different settings. These are called analogue devices.

Many arcade games use flashing lights and sounds to add excitement. Sometimes these sequences respond to user interaction, but often they just follow a predetermined control sequence.

Types of control system

Basically there are three different types of control system.
1. Systems controlled by a simple electronic circuit. These systems do not change once written and require no user interaction.
   For example an advertising LCD display will need to have a program written to determine the picture order, and the time each one is displayed for.

Task 1

Think about the different control systems that are used in IT based games.

- Open **Resource 5.4 Computer games** and complete the table.

2 Systems that use a computer program that has been written to control the sequence of events. These systems require a single input to activate the sequence of events.

For example an advertising billboard only requires a simple circuit containing a switch, like a light sensor, to turn the lighting on when it gets dark.

3 Systems that allow continual user interaction. They respond in a number of different ways depending on user interaction. These systems require a more complex program.

A railway platform information system requires continual interaction with the station manager, to keep the information up to date.

Task 2

Open **Resource 5.4 Control systems 1**.

Examples of the three different types of control system are given in the table. Think of one more example of each type of control system that are used in everyday life, and add your three examples to the table.

Displays used in control systems

Displays used in control systems need to be clear and able to respond quickly to changes in data.

The most commonly used display system is the one used on calculators and roadside information systems. These use a basic matrix of lit panels that can display any letter or number.

The simple number matrix consists of seven lines, which can be lit in a number of different ways to display all numbers.

Unit 5.4

Mimic software

A mimic is a control simulation. Mimics are often used in the design of complex control systems. Using a mimic has three main advantages.

1 It allows programmers to develop and test software before the system is built.
2 It minimises testing costs.
3 It can highlight any changes that need to be made to the product design before it has been built.

A simple mimic is included as part of the Flowol simulation software package, which your school may have a copy of.

▶ Skills help

Loading mimics into Flowol, pages 173–174.

Module Task

The simple number matrix display unit could act as a large count down timer for your game. A more complex system could have letters and could be used as an advertising display unit to promote your web game.

1 Work out how the numbers from 0 to 9 could be created using a basic seven-line matrix.

2 Write a program that would display each number in turn by controlling seven output channels that will turn on each of the seven lines.

You can complete this task in one of three ways depending on what facilities you have available.

 a If you have access to Flowol, use the mimic in **Resource 5.4 Matrix** and write a program to display each of the numbers on the matrix.
 b If you have an interface with a control program. Then you could make a model matrix, like the one shown.
 c If you do not have access to mimic or control software, then you can create a flowchart that demonstrates your solution assuming that you have seven outputs. Provide a sketch diagram labelling each line with the output channel it is controlled by.

3 When you have succeeded with the first program, modify the program to allow the user to start the count down by pressing a start button.

Task 3

1 How would you change the seven-line matrix to display all the letters in the alphabet?
2 How many output channels would you need to control this unit?
3 Sketch out your matrix solution.

Unit 5.4

Controlling events

Most control systems have a predetermined sequence of events, or the events are started by a single user input, for example a pelican crossing.

A computer program is written to control these events. Once fully tested the program is transferred to an EPROM (**E**rasable **P**rogrammable **R**ead **O**nly **M**emory chip).

The chip is then built into the electrical circuit. This enables systems like pelican crossings to operate without the expense and maintenance problems of computers.

'Bet these chips aren't too tasty!'

Task 4

Open **Resource 5.4 Control systems 2**.

Take the list of control systems you created in Task 1 and add them under the correct heading in the table.

Then add any new items you can think of now as a result of the other work you have done in this unit.

Task 5

Open **Resource 5.4 Sequencing**.

It is important to work out the sequence of events that you want to happen at each stage of your game.

1. Web based games are generally controlled by a mouse. Work out the sequence of events that happens when you visit a website of your choice.
   - What do you click on?
   - What happens when you do click?
   - What is the outcome of a click?

2. When you have worked out the sequence of events, write them down as a sequence of instructions and give them to a partner.

   Ask them to follow the instructions carefully and to make notes about what happens.

3. Did they get the same results as you?

Test centre

1. How many types of control system can you name? What are they?
2. What is a matrix?
3. What is an EPROM?

Unit 5.5
Creating an interactive control system

In this unit you are going to design an interactive control system for a promotional display unit, to advertise your web game.

Promotional display

You have two options for the promotional display unit you are going to create. You can either:

- create pages that provide information about the game
- or create pages that provide additional background information about the characters you have included in the game.

In each case the user will be able to decide what information he or she wants to access.

You will be using the same technology to control the display as would be used to control arcade games. You are going to use Mimic Creator (published by Data Harvest) to develop a system that uses screen based control (mouse) or, if you have a control interface, a number of push switches. You will also need a copy of Data Harvest's Flowol to run the mimic you have created.

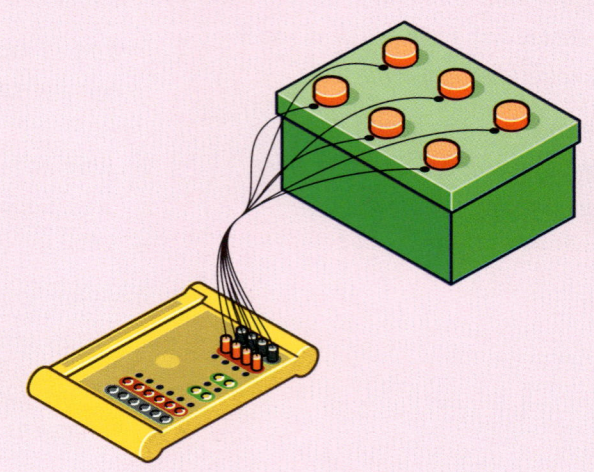

▶ **Skills help**

Using a control interface to produce an interactive information system, pages 174–175.

Unit 5.5

Interactive display units

Any information system should be designed to allow users to access the information they want as quickly as possible. Research has shown that if people do not get the information they want within three mouse clicks, or three button pushes, they walk away.

Control systems that are in an unsupervised area need to be as sescure as possible. By using a switch panel connected to an interface, as the method of user interaction, you increase the security of the system. This is because you can now remove the keyboard and mouse.

Task 1

Decide what type of interactive system you want to develop:
- promotional information about the game
- background information about the characters.

1. Plan the structure of the system. You should restrict yourself to a maximum of six pages of information.
2. Work out what information will go on each page. Try to keep the text you use to a minimum. A good guide is not to use more than 50 words per page.
3. Decide on the images you are going to use.
4. Prepare all the text files and images and place them in a single area on your computer or school network.

Creating mimics

In Unit 5.4 you used a ready prepared mimic to display the numbers on a seven-line matrix. You are now going to create your own mimic to demonstrate the type of control system you would use for your interactive display system.

The mimic software works with a single background picture and up to six more pictures that can be overlaid on the background image. Each of these pictures is linked to a particular output channel.

Task 2

Use any painting package you are familiar with to create the background image. (The picture size must be 400 × 320 pixels.)

You should consider your audience and ensure that your design is attractive to that audience.

You may wish to create frames for the pictures, and areas where the text can be displayed.

Save the file in .bmp format.

▶ Skills help

Creating a picture 400 × 320 using Windows Paint, page 175.

Using an interface with the Flowol software, pages 174–175.

Unit 5.5

Module Task

1 You are now going to create the six pages of information that will contain the text and images you produced in Task 1

The best way to do this is to add the information and images to a copy of the background image you created in Task 2, and save the completed page with a new name.

2 Save all your completed pages into a new folder within the mimic folder on your computer or school network.

3 Use **Resource 5.5 Mimics and channels** to help you create your own mimic and set each one against an output channel.

▶ *Skills help*

Creating mimics, pages 175–176.

Test centre

1 What is mimic software used for?
2 What are image attributes?
3 What are output channels?

Unit 5.6
Programming and testing the solution

In this unit you are going to write a program using Flowol to control a mimic.

The mimic you are going to use has three pages of information about some of the characters in a game. Each page is linked to an output channel – outputs 1, 2 and 3. You will use the on-screen input simulation to allow the user to select the page that they want to see. If you have a suitable interface, you could use a number of switches to control the mimic

Building computer programs

When creating computer programs it is good practice to build the program in small sections, often referred to as procedures or sub routines. Each section should be tested separately before being joined together to form the complete solution.

Task 1

You are now going to write a simple program to test the mimic you have created or the mimic in **Resource 5.6 Game 2a**.

1 To use your mimic load Flowol. Click on the **Window** drop down menu, and select your mimic. (You may be asked about default palettes, just click on **OK**.)
2 Create a copy of the program shown here.
3 Run the program.

The program should continually loop around the top half of the program. As soon as you run the program the input and output control box is displayed.

Clicking in the **Input 1** box has the same effect as pushing a switch on an interface box. When you click in the **Input 1** box, the page linked to **Output channel 1** should be displayed.

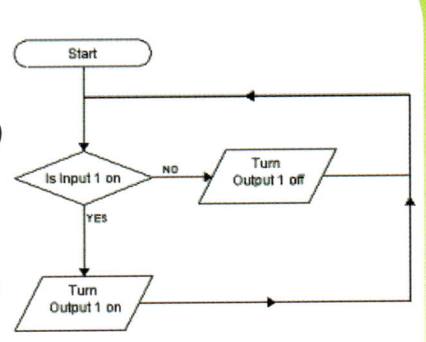

4 Now check that each of the other pages work correctly by editing the program to use different input and output channels.

Unit 5.6

Task 2

1. So that the user of the program knows which page is linked to which input channel, add a text box to the page, next to the flowchart, listing which character is linked to which input channel.

   Do this by:
   - Clicking close to where you want the text to appear.
   - Clicking on the **T** icon on the left hand side of the screen.
   - Entering a single line of text.

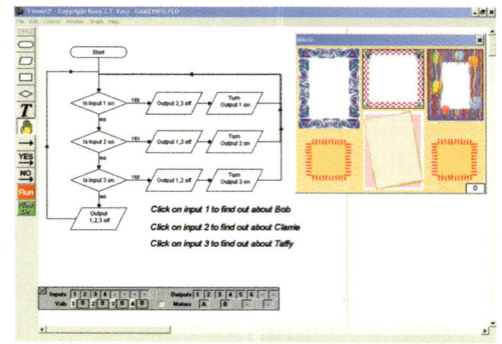

2. Repeat this process until all the information required has been added to the page.

Timing

In this example of a control system we need to continually check the status of the input devices, because we need to display the information requested as quickly as possible.

Some control systems may not need to check input devices as often. For example, heating systems work more efficiently if they are not continually turned on and off. Most central heating systems are designed to maintain a temperature within a range of four degrees. As room temperatures do not change quickly it may only be necessary to check the temperature sensors every 10 minutes.

So when designing control systems we should consider how often we need to capture data to run an efficient system.

Consider how often you would need to capture data for each of these situations: a greenhouse heater; a life support machine; an electronic breaking system; and a wind direction sensor that controls a wind turbine generator.

Module Task

1. Work with a partner to create a single program that will display each page of information.

   Each page will need to be linked to a single input channel.

2. When you have completed the program, test it and ask other people in your group to test your program and you test theirs.

Task 3

Adding the mimics to the web game would mean that all users would need the software to run the game.

1. Try to persuade the local community group that this would be a good idea by writing a brief description of how the web game would be made more interesting with the control aspects in place.

2. Use screenshots showing the increased interactivity that is available through the control screens and use of mimics.

3. Use a program like MS PowerPoint to annotate each of the screenshots with a description of what it allows the user to do and the benefits to the web game as a whole.

Test centre

1. How should people build computer programs?
2. What is a loop in a program?
3. What are input channels?

Unit 5.7
Marketing the product

In this unit you are going to identify the different methods of marketing the web game to the target audience. You will develop some direct marketing materials and use mail merge to contact your target audience..

How, where and when

The web game has been developed for a special age group and purpose, but how will anyone find out about it?

Marketing a product or service can be done in a number of different ways. Common marketing methods are all around us, like posters, billboards, TV advertisements, newspaper and magazine advertisements, radio jingles and tunes. One of the most common methods used today is direct mail, fax or text messages.

Some marketing methods are not so obvious. When you buy items from shops you normally end up carrying a carrier bag - and what is on the outside of the bag? The company's name. This is a method of marketing. Other forms of marketing include free gifts, T-shirts and badges.

Task 1

Open **Resource 5.7 Marketing**.

1 Over the next two days make a list of the different methods of marketing that you come across from morning until night.

2 Which methods did you pay the most attention to?

3 Were there any of the methods that you found annoying?

4 Would any of the methods be suitable for your web game?

161

Unit 5.7

Identify the target audience

To market items effectively it is necessary to make sure that the information reaches the correct audience.

Would giving a free cuddly toy to a middle aged man be an effective marketing method?

If you thought that the answer is no…what if the middle aged man also had a young family with him?

'So we've got a free clock, mug, calculator, notebook, pen, toy, tea towel, T-shirt…found anything you want to buy?'

So it is not only a case of getting the marketing method correct, but also getting the audience that will receive the materials correct.

Task 2

1 How can you find information about the target audience for the web game?

Remember: The target audience is people of your own age, not only in your school, but anywhere in the local community.

2 The Data Protection Act might make it more difficult. Why?

> Schools have to be very careful about the information they store about pupils and the way it is used.

Direct marketing

In Module 3 you learnt how companies buy lists of names and addresses and send marketing messages to them by mail, telephone, fax, email and text messaging. You also learnt about the various ways in which the law helps to protect people from receiving unwanted messages.

Almost all direct marketing messages are ignored by the recipient. So why do companies continue to send them? The answer is because the people who do respond can be put on the company's own database and the company can contact them regularly with information about new products. People who have actually asked to be put on the mailing list are far more likely to purchase products from the company.

Mail merge

The process of storing names and addresses in a database and merging them into individualised letters, labels, emails or faxes is called mail merge.

All you need in order to do a mail merge is a computer with word processing and database software, and a laser printer. Many people use mail merge at home, for example to do Christmas card labels. The data, such as names and addresses, can be stored in the word processing program, or in spreadsheet and database programs, such as MS Excel and MS Access.

▶ *Skills help*

Carrying out a mail merge, pages 176–177.

Module Task

1. Imagine you are going to hold a presentation evening to launch your web game. Using a word processing program write a description of the web game, using not more than 50 words, that could be used on a flyer for the presentation evening.

2. Save this file.

   The following community groups are to be contacted about the web game.
   - Under 16 year olds who are members of local youth clubs.
   - The youth leaders in four local community action groups.
   - All of the members of the overseas links organisations who are under 16.

3. What information do you need to know about this audience before they can be contacted through a mass mailing?

4. Is there a problem with the Data Protection Act?

   Look at **Resource 5.7 Contacts**. This shows you how data to be used in a mass mailing can be stored.

5. Use mail merge to produce a series of labels for these contacts so that information about the game can be sent to them.

6. Create a second data file that could be used to store new contact details of other groups that could also be interested in attending the presentation evening.

Unit 5.7

Task 3

Using mail merge you can insert items of data from a data file into the body of a document.

1 Create an invitation to the presentation evening where the names of the people being invited are automatically inserted into an invitation like the one below. The names would be in place of the XXXs.

> **Special Invite for XXX**
>
> Hello XXX
>
> You are invited to come along to an evening of entertainment where you will have the chance to try our new web game.
>
> XXX, as a special treat you are also offered a set of the promotional materials that are available to accompany the game.

2 Open **Resource 5.7 Contacts**. Delete the names that are in the file and add the details of people in your class who you would invite to the evening. Save the file.

3 Create a set of invitations for the people in your class, making use of mail merge to insert their names.

Task 4

Open **Resource 5.7 Promotional materials**.

The marketing campaign is going to make use of a set of five items for marketing the web game. These are:
- a poster
- a web game website map
- a logo design
- stationery - letterhead, business cards
- a web game cheat sheet

Sketch out ideas for each of these items.

Test centre

1 What is a target audience?
2 What does mail merge do?
3 What does the Data Protection Act do for people?

Unit 5.8
Developing and evaluating a marketing package

In this unit you are going to create the materials that could be used in a marketing package using a range of appropriate software. You will get feedback from end users to improve your marketing materials.

Corporate look and feel

In *ICT Matters 1* you learnt about corporate image and how it is used to promote a company or organisation.

The web game needs to be given a corporate image, so that any items to be included in a marketing package will have the same look and feel as the website that you have created.

You need to think about:
- What are the most important facts about the web game?
- What age group should be attracted to the game?
- What are the main features of the game, for example what is on the separate pages?
- What level of language should be used, remember some of the audience may not use English as their first language.
- What is the purpose of the web game?

165

Unit 5.8

Task 1

> Open **Resource 5.8 Corporate image**.

1 Create a list of five points that you think are the most important aspects of the web game.

This should help you to identify the type of corporate image that is needed.

2 Sketch out ideas for the type of logo you could create for the web game, which meets all of the points that you have listed.

3 Annotate your sketch to show how it relates to the web game. For example where you selected similar fonts and colours, where the shape or style of the layout is similar.

Selecting software for developing marketing materials

Some types of software can be used to do several different jobs, but it is important to make sure that the correct type of software is selected for the task that is being carried out.

Remember what happened to the file size when a word processing program was used to create an HTML document? Because it is not the best software for designing web pages, the file size was very large. When the correct software was selected the file size was much smaller.

In the same way software for designing the marketing materials should be selected carefully.

Graphic images, such as logos, should be designed in an art graphics program or scanned in from an original drawing.

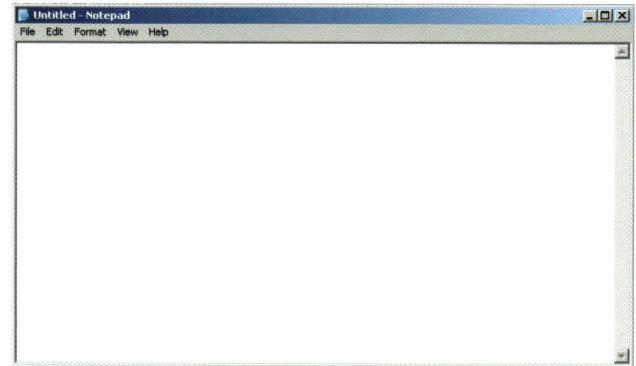

Text for documents should be created in a text editing program, such as a Notepad or a word processing program, and then copied and pasted into other documents when needed.

Posters, leaflets, and business cards should be designed in an art or graphics program, or a desktop publishing program.

Task 2

Open Resource 5.8 Software.

1. What type of software will you use to create the materials for the marketing package?

2. List the order in which you will create the materials, making sure that you have designed any items that will be used on any of the others in the correct order.

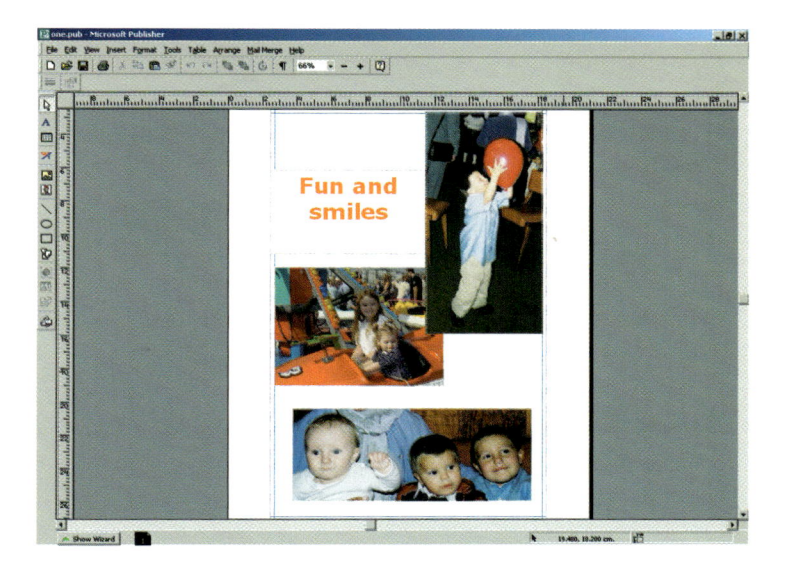

Fitness for purpose

Before you can create the promotional materials you need to consider their fitness for purpose. You have already thought about matching the items content and layout to the audience, but what about the way in which they will be used?

- Which items will be handled and need to be protected or produced in a way to help them last longer?
- Which items will only be looked at?
- Which items will need to be printed?

Module Task

1. Using your planned order of production from Task 2, create the materials for the marketing package.

2. Before you begin each item, make sure that you have completed an annotated sketch that gives details of why the item is to look as planned.

3. If you have to change the order in which you work, make alterations to your planning table completed in Task 2.

4. When you have completed the materials, select five people from your class to trial the web game and receive the marketing materials.

   Open Resource 5.8 Product and marketing evaluation.

5. Note their comments and what changes to the marketing and promotional materials would be desirable as a result of the comments made.

Unit 5.8

Task 3

1. Create a data file that holds the details of the five people you have selected to trial you web game.
2. Personalise the marketing materials that you produce where relevant with the names from the data file.
3. Does this make the materials more appealing to them?
4. Is it possible to personalise their use of the web game?
5. Describe any websites that you know that allow you to personalise the way that they are displayed.

Task 4

A presentation folder needs to be put together to hold a project report. This folder will contain a description of all the stages of the web game project, along with screenshots of the website and a copy of the web game on CD-ROM or floppy disk.

Design the front cover of a folder that could be used to hold:
- A Project report covering the analysis, design and creation of the web game.
- A copy of the web game on floppy disc or CD-ROM.
- Future plans for development.

Test centre

1. What is a corporate image?
2. Why does it matter which software is used to develop different types of materials?
3. What does fitness for purpose mean?

Unit 5.9
Producing the project report

In this unit you are going to create a project report on the stages of development used in the web game, and how you used data and skills from all the other units to help you to produce an integrated system.

Project report

Remember the web game is a system!

The project report will be presented in a folder and will contain:

- A report on the *analysis* of the system, including a feasibility report and details of what the system needs to do.
- A report on the *design* of the system, including how the system actually works.
- A report on the *implementation* of the system, including details of what had to be created to make it work, how this was done, and how data files were integrated into the sytstem. There should be a copy of the website on a CD-ROM or floppy disk.
- A report on the *testing* of the system.
- A report on how the system could be made more interactive for a user through control software programming (you have this already from Unit 5.6).
- A report on the *marketing and promotion* of the system, including the marketing package and feedback from users on the performance of the final system (you have this already from Unit 5.8).

Design of the report

The different reports do not have to be long. They should just give a summary of the most important facts about the stages of development (life cycle) of the web game system, and the marketing and promotion of the web game.

Task 1

Open **Resource 5.9 Project report**.

To prepare for writing your project report, complete a table that lists the development work you have carried out.

Some of the sections in the table have been started for you, but you will need to add your own filenames and resources used.

Folder presentation

The project report is to be presented in a folder. The presentation folder could be in many different formats including:

- Ring binder – where the pages are hole punched or are placed in plastic wallets.
- Folded cardboard – where there is a 'pocket' produced for the separate sheets of paper and a holder for a floppy disc or CD-ROM.
- Envelope file – practical and cheap.

The number of pages and other items to be stored is a good guide in choosing the best folder format. A cardboard folder with too many pieces of paper might cause problems as the pages could fall out. A ring binder with too few pages could be too expensive.

Template file

In order to make sure that all the separate reports look the same and can be contained in the folder that will hold the project report, a template file needs to be created.

A template file allows you to set up the page layout, including the margins, font and styles used. The content is then entered into the template and the file is saved with a different name, keeping the template file for use with another report.

Within a template file it is important to set up the properties of any tables to be used.

Task 2

1. Estimate the number of pieces of paper you are going to produce in the project report.
2. Try out this number of pages in each of the types of folder that are available to you.
3. Which one will be best for the way you want the project report to be presented?
4. Make a decision as to the type of folder that will be used - this is important, as it will affect the way in which you set up the layout of the reports.

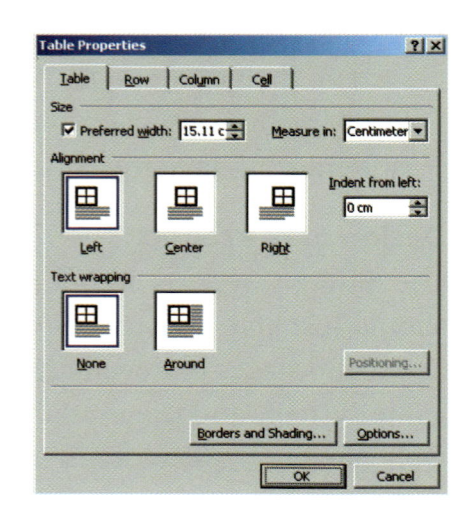

Unit 5.9

Module Task

1. Create a template file in a word processing program that you can use to produce the separate reports in your project report.

   Make sure that you have set up:
   - page layout
   - fonts to be used
   - styles to be used
   - table properties.

   Do you want to include headers and footers?

   Are the reports going to have page numbers that continue from one report to the next, or are the reports going to be numbered separately?

   Do the reports all have the same title and use different sections headings?

2. Save your template file.

3. Use your template file to create each separate report. Use the table you created in Task 2 to help you to write the content of each report.

▶ Skills help

Creating a template file, page 178.

Task 3

Open **Resource 5.9 Evaluation criteria**.

Use this template to help you create a list of criteria that you can use to evaluate the following aspects of the final system:

The design of the web game – layout of the web pages
   – look of the web pages.
The content of the web game – how up to date the information is
   – how easy it was to find the information.
How user friendly the web game is – more interactivity needed
   – more user instructions about the web game.

Unit 5.9

Task 4

You are going to produce a customer satisfaction chart to be included in your project report.

The chart should be linked to a database, like the chart shown. This is so that the chart is automatically updated when more users evaluate the system and their data is entered into the database.

1 Create a data capture sheet for users to complete based upon the evaluation criteria developed in Task 3. This could be on paper or it could be saved in electronic format for users to complete on a computer. Remember the data needs to be in numeric format if you are going to create charts from it. So you might want to use a points ranking system.

2 Create a database in a spreadsheet program to store the responses of users.

3 Create the chart and paste it into your project report so that it will automatically update.

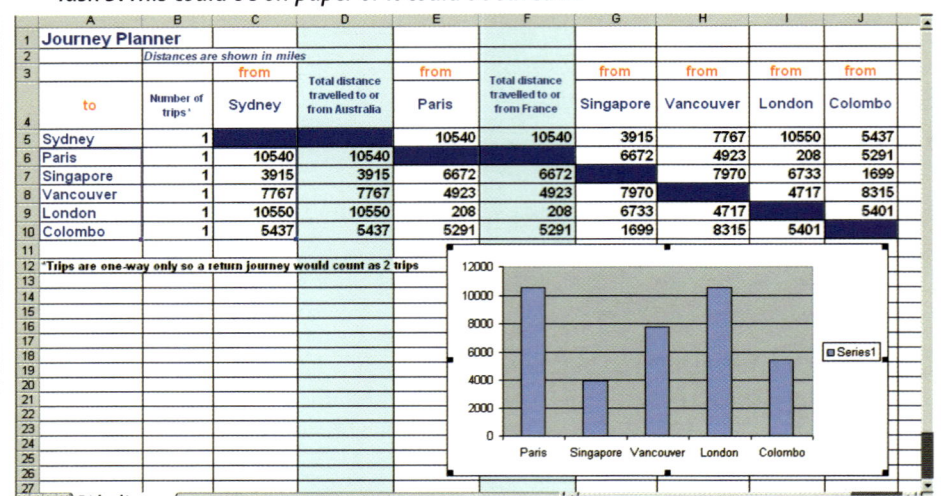

Remember: You should make the data collection form easy to fill in. You also need to make sure that your questions will give you data that can be presented in chart format, for example the answers might need to be yes or no.

Make the questions reflect your web game and not be too general, it is your system that is being evaluated.

Test centre

1 What are the development stage of a project or system?
2 What is a template file?
3 How can data be entered into a report so that it will update automatically?

Module 5 — Skills help

Creating a time line for development

An effective way to create a timeline for the development of a website is to use project management software.

Another way that works just as well is to use a spreadsheet set up with dates in the worksheet. Each cell represents a day, month or year depending on how long the development is going to take.

1. Open a new worksheet in a spreadsheet application.
2. Select the row where the dates for the project will be displayed.
3. Go to **Format** and select **Cells**.

4. In the **Format Cells** dialogue box, select **Custom** and scroll down until you find **dd-mmm** (Date and Month).

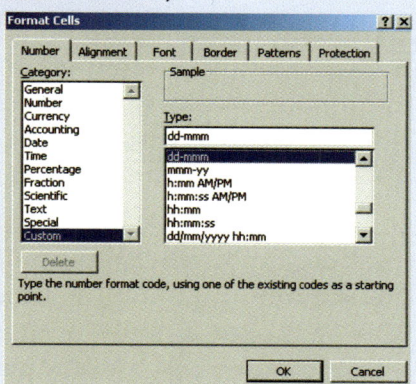

5. Enter the first date of the development project into the first cell.

With the cell formatted for a date, if you enter 3/5, the date 03 May appears.

6. Enter the second date in the next cell.

7. Split the date rows on the worksheet up into separate months if needed.
8. Enter the details of the different items to be developed in column A.
9. Fill with colour the cells under the dates that will be used for their development.

This gives an easy to understand time line for the different stages of the website.

The length of the stages of development can be increased or decreased.

Loading mimics into Flowol

1. Load Flowol.
2. Click on the **Windows** menu and select **Mimics**.
3. A list will be displayed. Select the mimic you want to use and click **OK**.  
4. The mimic will usually be displayed on the right hand side of the screen.

173

Skills 5

Transferring the mimic from the Resource CD to your computer

Mimics are stored in a folder called MIMICS on a computer. This is in the FLOWOL folder. There is a separate folder for each mimic inside the MIMICS folder. These folders contain the images used by each mimic.

There are a number of programs within the FLOWOL folder that contain information that links each image to an input or output channel.

To transfer the mimic from the Resource CD you need to copy:

- the folder containing the images, called **Resource 5.4 Matrix**, inside the MIMICS folder
- and the program called **Resource 5.4 Numtest** within the FLOWOL directory.

All these files appear in the folder called FLOWOL on the Resource CD.

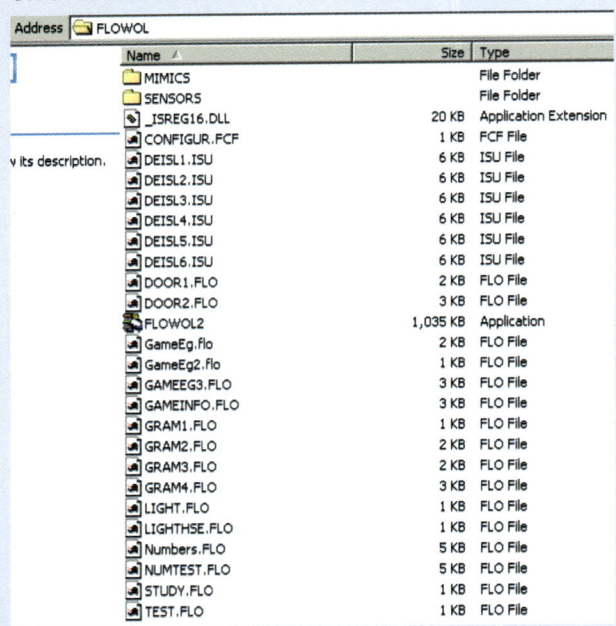

Name	Size	Type
MIMICS		File Folder
SENSORS		File Folder
_ISREG16.DLL	20 KB	Application Extension
CONFIGUR.FCF	1 KB	FCF File
DEISL1.ISU	6 KB	ISU File
DEISL2.ISU	6 KB	ISU File
DEISL3.ISU	6 KB	ISU File
DEISL4.ISU	6 KB	ISU File
DEISL5.ISU	6 KB	ISU File
DEISL6.ISU	6 KB	ISU File
DOOR1.FLO	2 KB	FLO File
DOOR2.FLO	3 KB	FLO File
FLOWOL2	1,035 KB	Application
GameEg.flo	2 KB	FLO File
GameEg2.flo	1 KB	FLO File
GAMEEG3.FLO	3 KB	FLO File
GAMEINFO.FLO	3 KB	FLO File
GRAM1.FLO	1 KB	FLO File
GRAM2.FLO	2 KB	FLO File
GRAM3.FLO	2 KB	FLO File
GRAM4.FLO	3 KB	FLO File
LIGHT.FLO	1 KB	FLO File
LIGHTHSE.FLO	1 KB	FLO File
Numbers.FLO	5 KB	FLO File
NUMTEST.FLO	5 KB	FLO File
STUDY.FLO	1 KB	FLO File
TEST.FLO	1 KB	FLO File

Using a control interface to produce an interactive information system

You must first tell the FLOWOL software which interface you are using and how it is connected to your computer.

1. Select **Interface** from the **Control** menu.

2. A rather complex looking window will be displayed. To make it work you must have one of the interfaces listed on the right hand side of the screen.

3. Select the interface you are going to use.

4. You have to tell the software where the interface box is plugged in. Usually it will be one of the serial ports called COM 1, COM 2, COM 3.

5. Select the port you have connected the interface to.

If you don't know which number then it's a case of trail and error. Try COM 1, if that doesn't work try COM 2 and so on. If you are using a laptop then there is probably only one COM port, and the others will be greyed out, as in the image above.

6. When you have selected all the options, click **OK** and **Save**.

7 You should get the following messaged displayed.

Message from Flowol: To make the interface operational click on 'Simulate' in the 'Control' menu to remove the tick.

This is just a reminder to turn the program from simulate mode into control mode.

8 Follow the instructions and you are away!

NB. If you are using a USB interface like FLOWGO you should look at the manual as the settings have to be set up differently.

Creating a picture 400 × 320 using Windows Paint

The background picture that you are going to use in your mimic must be 400 × 320 pixels and saved in BMP format.

Most art packages will allow you to resize pictures, but it is better to start with a blank canvas the right size as reducing or enlarging pictures can result in a loss of quality.

Windows Paint allows you to save files in BMP format and create a picture to a particular pixel size, but it will not resize pictures.

1 Click on the **Images** menu and select **Attributes**.
2 Enter 400 in the **Width** box and 320 in the **Height** box and make sure the **pixels** option is selected.

Creating mimics

1 Load the mimic software
2 Click on the green folder icon
3 Click on the folder containing your images.

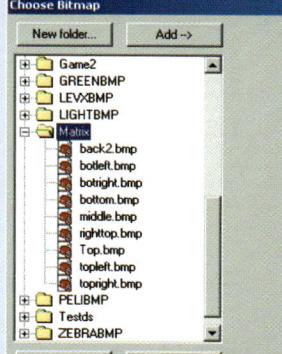

4 The images will now be displayed.

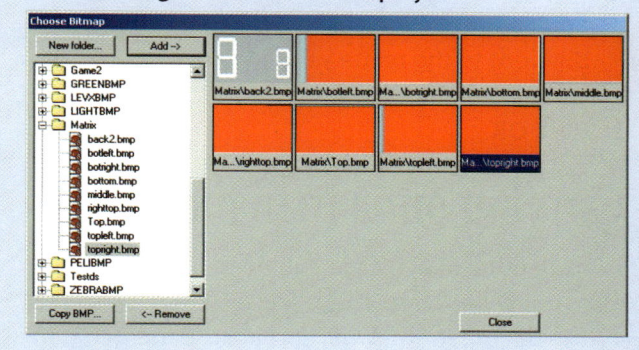

5 Highlight each image you need and click on the **Add** button.
6 When you have added all the images, click on **Close**.

Linking pictures to an output channel

1 Click on the **Out** icon.
2 On the top tool bar the following dialogue box will be displayed.

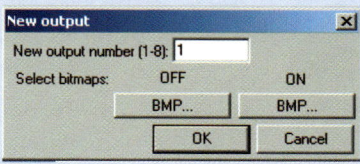

3 Decide which image you want to link to output channel 1.
4 When you click on the **BMP** button below **ON**, all the images you have selected will be displayed.

5 Click on the image you want to use and click **OK**.

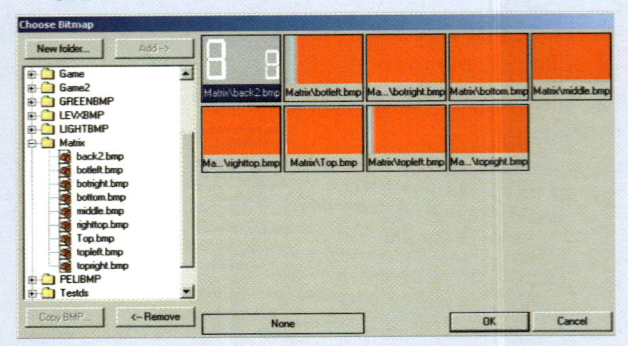

6 Repeat this process for each image until you have an output channel allocated to each image.

Saving a mimic

1 Select **File** from the menu and click **Save as**.
2 Enter a name for your mimic. The name must be different to the name you gave to the folder containing your images.
3 Click **OK**.

Carrying out a mail merge

To carry out a mail merge you need to have two main items prepared. These are:
- the document that will contain the merged data
- the database containing the data to be merged.

The first dialogue box that appears controls the way that the mail merge is carried out. You can create your database and document from this dialogue box.

1 Go to **Tools** on the menu bar, and select **Mail Merge**.

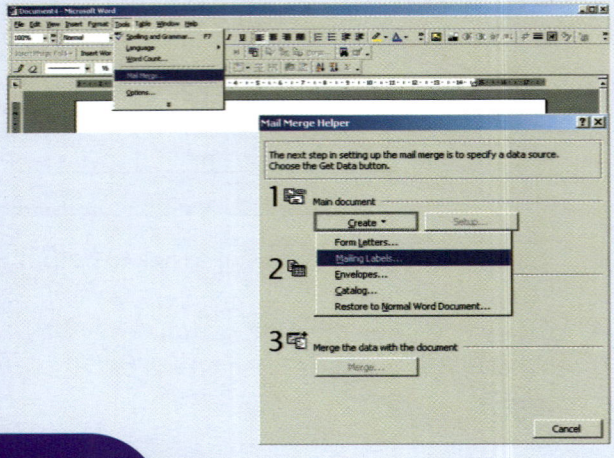

2 The **Mail Merge Helper** dialogue box appears.
3 Click the **Create** button and choose the type of document that you want, for example mailing labels.
4 Another dialogue box then appears, giving you the choice of using the document you have open already for the mail merge, or creating a new one. Click on **Change Document Type** to continue.

5 Click on the **Get Data** button under **Data Source**.
6 Select **Create Data Source** if you do not already have one already prepared. Select **Open Data Source** if you already have one.

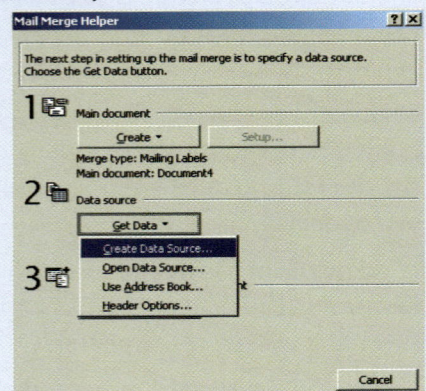

Creating a data source

1 Select all of the fields that you want to appear in the merged document.
2 Remove any fields that you do not want with the << tool.

The structure of the database is complete, but you are warned that at the moment there is no data in it.

3 Select **Edit Data Source** to add data into the database.

4 You can enter the data into the separate fields for all the people you want to send information to.

5 Select **View Source** to check the details that have been entered, this appears as a table in a Word document.

Set up the main document

1 A warning box appears that allows you to set up the main document.

2 Select the type of document that it is.

3 Select the position and layout for how the fields should be printed.

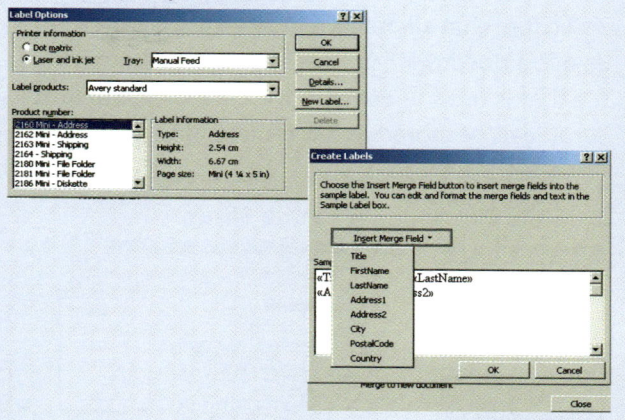

4 Select the way that you want the merge to happen.

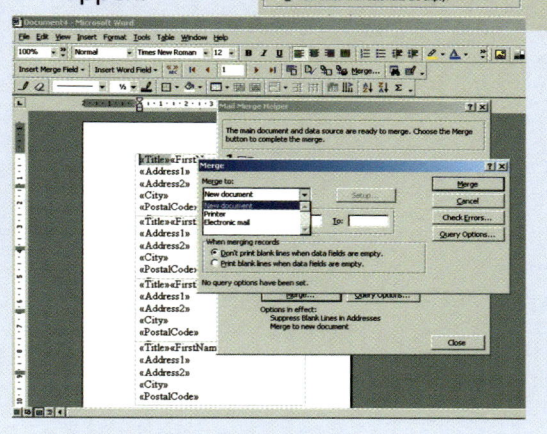

5 You can see the layout of the merged fields behind the dialogue boxes.

6 Click the **Merge** button.

The merged document appears.

Skills 5

177

Skills 5

Creating a template file

To ensure that all documents look the same, or to re-use a document style over and over again, the file that is used to develop the correct layout and setup can be stored as a template file.

1. Open a new word processing document.
2. Go to **File** and select **Page Setup**.

3. Set the margins, paper size and orientation, the printer and any layout details that are special for the document.

4. Set any headers, footers and place any text and images that you would like to appear each time the document is used.
5. When you have finished go to **File**, and select **Save As**.
6. In the **Save as type** box, select **Document Template**.
7. Enter the file name and click **OK**.

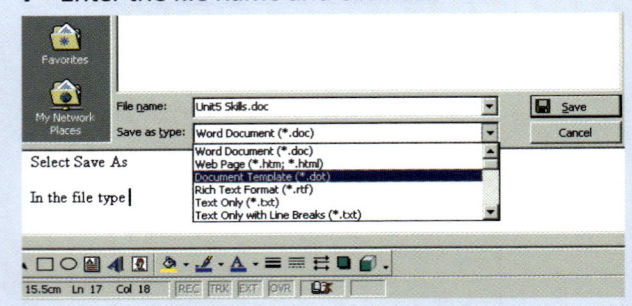

The file will now have an extension of *.dot* instead of *.doc*.

Glossary

Accessible	To make something easy to understand by a number of people.
ADSL	Asymmetric Digital Subscriber Line – a type of broadband connection to the Internet.
Analogue	A type of signal that varies continuously.
Appraise	To examine something and judge it.
Assumption	To think something is true without having any proof that it is.
Authentic	If something is true, or is what people say it is, then it is called authentic.
Bandwidth	The difference between the highest and lowest frequencies for a transmission channel. Sometimes this term is used to talk about the amount of data that can be sent through a communication channel in a second, but this is incorrect and should be called data rate.
Bias	To support or argue against something in an unfair way because you believe in something, and do not give the opposite point of view.
Body text	The main text in a document.
Boolean connector	The use of AND, OR and NOT in a search that will have two possible outcomes, true or false.
Broadband	A communication connection that has a download speed of greater than 56kbps (kilobytes per second).
Continuous	Without stopping – a continuous signal is one that does not have any breaks in it.
Copy	As well as being used to refer to a second version of an image, text or file, the word 'copy' is sometimes used to describe the text in a newspaper article.
Data Protection Act	Legislation that provides security to an individual about how companies and organisations can use their personal data.
Datalogging	A system that connects sensors through a control interface to a computer system. The datalogging system is used to monitor physical events over a period of time and send the changes in data to the computer for analysis.
Dial-up	A temporary connection between a computer and the Internet through a modem.
Digital	A type of communication where data is transferred through a sequence of signals, as in binary data.
Drop-down menu	A list of choices that appears when a user clicks on a selection box or downward arrow.
Dry run	To try something out before it is used within a live system.
Dynamic link	A link between two sources of data, perhaps a web page table and a word document, that allows data in the file to be automatically updated.
Feasible	Something that can be done or achieved.
File extension	The ending of a computer file that shows what type of file it is. For example, *.doc* is a MS Word file, *.xls* is a MS Excel file, *.bmp* is a Bitmapped graphic file.
File size	The amount of disk space that a file takes up when stored on a computer system, measured in kilobytes (Kb) or megabytes (Mb).
Financial model	A spreadsheet model that is used to work out complex calculations and can be used to work out budgets and expenditure.
Flyer	A brief document that provides information to a target group of people.

Glossary

Forecast	A report that shows what is likely to happen in the future, for example a weather forecast.
Function	An instruction or procedure that will carry out a calculation, search or sort to produce a new value.
Goal seek	A software tool that works out the best solution to a problem in a model.
Hacking	Accessing a computer without the permission of the user. This could be done through the Internet or through programs that allow other users access to passwords that have been set on a system.
Hierarchy	A structure that can be used to organise files or web pages so that there is one main access point at the top and several things connected below.
Hypertext	A term used for documents that contain links that allow a user to move easily from one section of text to another.
Hypertext mark-up language (HTML)	A computer language that can be used to set up web pages. The code sets out the way the web page will appear in terms of fonts, font sizes, tables and images. It also allows for hyperlinks to be created between web pages.
Integrated Services Digital Network (ISDN)	A method of connecting a computer to the Internet that allows a single wire to carry voice and digital signals at the same time.
Length delimited file	A file that contains data that has been split up by a series of symbols, such as commas. A *.csv* file is a length delimited file.
Linear	This can be used to describe different things. A linear connection is one that involves a series of events, in which one follows the other directly. Linear length is to do with the length of an object, rather than the volume of it. A linear diagram is made up of lines.
Live data	Data that is frequently changing.
Misrepresentation	To give a false idea, opinion or description of someone.
Misuse	To use something in a way that was not intended.
Modem	An electronic device that converts the digital data from a computer into an analogue signal so that it can be transferred over a telephone line. It then changes the analogue signal from the telephone line into a digital signal so the computer can deal with it.
Modify	To change or improve something.
Monitor	To watch something carefully over a period of time, for example a datalogging system would 'monitor' physical changes in a situation.
Navigate	To find a way around something, for example finding the way to move between web pages.
Organise	To sort things out so they are easy to find or use.
Parameter	A set of facts or limits that sets out how something can or must happen.
Personal information	Details about individuals that are often stored on computer systems and might be useful to others, for example name, address, credit card details, health details.
Physical data	Something in the physical environment that can be measured, e.g. temperature, motion or light.
Plain Old Telephone System (POTS)	The traditional voice communication system provided by telephone companies.
Plausible	Something that is likely to be true or able to be achieved.
Public information system	A display in a public place to provide information, for example displays about flight arrivals and departures in an airport.

Glossary

Public Switched Telephone Network (PSTN)	The collection of interconnected communication systems used by a variety of telephone companies from around the world.
Random number generator	A software tool that can be used to generate a number from anywhere within a given range. For example it can generate a random series of numbers between 1 and 300, e.g. 15, 285, 64 and 172.
Readability	How easy it is to read something, for example whether the font and language are suitable for the target group.
Remote datalogging	A datalogging system that is set up to run automatically, away from any physical links to a computer system.
Remote sensor	Sensors that are put in place without any physical links to a datalogging system.
Rule	An instruction about what should be done, setting out the usual way to do it.
Sample rate	How frequently measurements are taken by a datalogging system.
Sequence of instructions	A list of instructions where each instruction follows on from the one before.
Serif/sans serif	A serif font is one that has decorative strokes at the end of the letter's main strokes. Whereas a sans serif font does not have these added strokes.
Site map	A chart that shows all the pages of a website in a list and gives details of what is on the separate pages.
Storyboard	A way to work out the sequence of events that should happen if someone uses or watches something, for example a cartoon can be drawn out using a storyboard.
Structure	The way the parts of something are arranged or put together.
Style sheet	A software file containing code that will set up the way a web page will look.
System life cycle	The different stages of developing a system, which form a complete cycle: identify and analyse, design, implement, test, evaluate.
Tags	The term used within HTML to describe a single element of code.
Threshold	The level at which something will start to happen.
Transmission speed	How fast a connection can transfer data.
Valid	Something that is based upon good reasons, or facts that can be proved to be true.
Web query	A way to set up a link between a spreadsheet file and an Internet website, so that data from the web page can be transferred directly into the spreadsheet.

Index

A
absolute cell references 118, 135
Access
 datasheet appearance 88, 105
 filtering 99–101
 reports 90, 106–7
 sorting 101
alphanumeric data 72
AND, OR and NOT in searches 72, 79–80, 97–8

B
background picture 175
bandwidth 40
bar charts 7
Boolean connectors 72, 79–80, 97–8

C
© symbol 77–8
cell references 72, 118, 135
charts displaying outputs 119
 editing 123, 134
 spreadsheets 27–9
 updating 120
collecting data 5
computer program creation 159–60
computer program timing 160
computer system 140
control interface 174–5
control systems 152–5
copyright 77–8
corporate image 165–7
CSV files 7, 24
customer satisfaction chart 172

D
data
 collection 5
 extraction 10
 Internet as source 9
 live 9–12
 manipulation 11
 presentation 7
 public information system 12
 storage 7
 types 72
data protection 91–4
data source for mail merge 176–7
databases
 fields 72
 filtering 72
 flat file 72, 83–4, 85
 linking tables 102–4
 queries 86
 relational 72, 84, 85
 relational, creating 101–4
 reports 89–90
 searches 72–3, 87–90
 sorting 72–3
 structure 83–6
 within spreadsheet 98
datalogging 3, 6
datasheets appearance 87–8, 104–5
development plan 142–4
development timeline 173
direct marketing 92–3, 162–3
display screens 16
drop–down lists 122, 133

E
encryption 128
EPROM 155
events sequence 140
Excel
 datasheet appearance 88, 104–5
 filtering 98–99
 reports 89, 106
 sorting 98

F
file properties 62–3
file saving 62
file size 62–3
filtering data 72
flowcharts 140
Flowol 173–4
forecasts 9
formulae
 basics 134
 brackets 134–5
 outline 110
 spreadsheets 112
Freedom of Information Act 2000: 91
FrontPage 66–9, 149

G
glossary 179–81
goal seek 113–14, 132–3

H
hackers 93
hierarchical diagrams 47–8
home page 45–6, 49–50
hotlinks iii
HTML
 background colour 61
 extra coding 42
 fonts 61
 outline 35, 37–8
 styles 61
 tags 61
 use for web pages 41
 using 61
hyperlinks 46–7, 63, 68–9
hypertext 68–9

I
information
 believability 74–5
 evaluating 74–8
 links 76–7
 opinions 75
 reliability 76
 searching databases 87–90
 searching for 79–82
 text searches 72
interactive display units 157
interactive information system 174–5
Internet
 data to spreadsheets 26–7
 definition 3
 search engines 81
 source of data 9

L
length delimited files 7
line graphs 7

Index

M

mail merge 163, 176–7
marketing a product 161–4
marketing package 165–8
marketing software 166–7
mimic
   creation 157, 175–6
   loading 173–4
   software 154
   transfer 174
Mimic Creator 156
model
   appearance 121–3
   definition 109, 127
   developing new model 116–20
   drop–down lists 122
   finding solutions 111–15
   improving 124
   inputs 117
   outputs 119–20
   preparation 116
   processing 117–18
   random numbers 124, 135–6
   reviewing 121
   universal 126

N

numeric data 72

P

passwords 127–8
personal information protection 91–2
pie charts 7
PowerPoint
   animation 31–2
   automating 32
   captions 31
   spreadsheet 30–1
   timing 32
presentation
   automating 32
   definition 3
   timing 32
   viewing 31–2
Privacy and Electronic Communications (EC Directive) Regulations 2003: 91, 94
project report 169–72
promotional display 156
public information system

adding information 16
automating 16–20
displaying data 14
evaluating 21–2
input 12, 14
output 14–15
processing information 14
volatile information 20

R

random numbers 110, 135–6
relative cell references 118, 135
reports
   creating 106–7
   databases 89–90
   results of search 89–90

S

search engines
   Boolean connectors 97–8
   Internet 81
searches
   Boolean connectors 72, 79–80
   computer system 81–2, 96–7
   contents 96
   names 96
   text 96
   wild card 81
sensors 3
sequencing of events 140
simulation
   control 154
   definition 109, 127
   universal 126
site map 55–6
slide show automation 17–19
solution testing 159–60
SPAM 93–4
spin doctoring 12
spreadsheets
   absolute cell references 118, 135
   cell references 72, 118, 135
   charts 27–9
   containing database 98
   copying data tables 26
   creating web queries 27
   data from Internet 26–7
   definition 3
   deleting data 26
   drop–down lists 133
   formulae 110, 112
   goal seek 132–3

importing CSV files 24
new entries 132
PowerPoint 30–1
relative cell references 118, 135
trial and improvement 132
workbooks 110
worksheet data 29–30
worksheet names 29
worksheets 110
style sheets
   editing 54, 69
   using 69
   web pages 51–2, 53–5
system
   automating a process 152–5
   control systems 152–5
   design 149–51
   development 149–51
   development plan 142–4
   feasibility study 141–4
   life cycle 139, 141
   modelling 145–8
   outline 139
   project report 169–72
   timeline 143–4

T

tables
   alignment 64
   borders 65
   cell spacing 65
   columns, width 64–5
   creating 63–4
   formatting 63–4
   rows, adding 65
   rows, height 64
target audience 162
template file 178
testing solutions 159–60
text searches 72, 96
timeline 143–4, 173
toolbars 24
transmission speed 40
trial and improvement 113–14, 132

U

URL 9

V

volatile information 20

Index

W

web design software
   adding items 68
   cells, borders 69
   cells, merging 67–8
   cells, size 67
   hyperlinks 68–9
   hypertext 68–9
   layout change 67
   outline 50–1
   system development 149–51
   tools 66
   using 66–9
   views 66
web game
   designing clues 150
   input 145–6
   marketing 161–4
   output 145–6
   process 145–6
   programming 156–8
   project report 169–72
   resources 146
   sample 145–6
   testing 159–60
web pages
   content 44–5
   designing 53–6
   extra coding 42
   file sizes 41
   HTML 41
   hyperlinks 46–7, 63
   navigation 63
   producing 40–2
   structure 49–52
   style sheets 51–2, 53–5
websites
   addresses 25
   appearance 43–4
   costs 147
   database supporting 129–30
   encryption 128
   evaluating 36, 57–9
   favourites 25
   hierarchical diagrams 47–8
   home page 45–6, 49–50
   links 76–7
   navigation 45
   outline 35
   passwords 127–8
   planning ahead 58–9
   saving addresses 25
   saving data 26–7
   site map 55–6
   structure 43–8
what if...questions 111
wild card searches 81
Windows Paint 175
workbooks 110
worksheets
   data copying 29–30
   definition 110
   renaming 29